Birder's Journal

NATIONAL
GEOGRAPHIC

WASHINGTON, D.C.

Contents

Checklist

This checklist is based on *The Check-list of North American Birds* (1998) that is prepared by the American Ornithologists' Union (A.O.U.). Since the A.O.U.'s checklist covers a larger geographic area than is covered in this guide, we have edited the list to include only those species that have been officially recorded in the continental United States and Canada as well as their adjacent waters.

Checklists are, by their nature, always evolving. New species are recorded, species are split into subspecies, introduced populations die out, or native species may become extinct. If you wish to keep up to date with the most current list, consult the supplements published by the A.O.U. or the most current edition of the American Birding Association's checklist.

To be of most use to birdwatchers, the National Geographic Society *Birder's Journal* sometimes includes species that are not found on the A.O.U. checklist. They may be naturally occurring species not yet on the list or exotic species that are regularly seen but not yet officially accepted.

This checklist also mentions some birds that our guide does not include. In general, these are accidental species, most with only one or two recent recordings.

(Adapted with permission from The A.O.U. Checklist of North American Birds, 7th Edition, 1998.)

Key: **BOLDFACE** indicates order.
CAPITALS indicate family.
Check boxes indicate individual species.

GAVIIFORMES

GAVIIDAE

☐ Red-throated Loon *Gavia stellata*
☐ Arctic Loon *Gavia arctica*
☐ Pacific Loon *Gavia pacifica*
☐ Common Loon *Gavia immer*
☐ Yellow-billed Loon *Gavia adamsii*

PODICIPEDIFORMES

PODICIPEDIDAE

☐ Least Grebe *Tachybaptus dominicus*
☐ Pied-billed Grebe *Podilymbus podiceps*
☐ Horned Grebe *Podiceps auritus*
☐ Red-necked Grebe *Podiceps grisegena*
☐ Eared Grebe *Podiceps nigricollis*
☐ Western Grebe *Aechmophorus occidentalis*
☐ Clark's Grebe *Aechmophorus clarkii*

PROCELLARIIFORMES

DIOMEDEIDAE

☐ Yellow-nosed Albatross *Thalassarche chlororhynchos*
☐ Shy Albatross *Thalassarche cauta*
☐ Black-browed Albatross *Thalassarche melanophris*
☐ Light-mantled Albatross *Phoebetria palpebrata*
☐ Wandering Albatross *Diomedea exulans*
☐ Laysan Albatross *Phoebastria immutabilis*
☐ Black-footed Albatross *Phoebastria nigripes*
☐ Short-tailed Albatross *Phoebastria albatrus*

PROCELLARIIDAE

☐ Northern Fulmar *Fulmarus glacialis*
☐ Herald Petrel *Pterodroma arminjoniana*
☐ Murphy's Petrel *Pterodroma ultima*
☐ Mottled Petrel *Pterodroma inexpectata*
☐ Black-capped Petrel *Pterodroma hasitata*
☐ Cook's Petrel *Pterodroma cookii*
☐ Stejneger's Petrel *Pterodroma longirostris*
☐ Streaked Shearwater *Calonectris leucomelas*
☐ Cory's Shearwater *Calonectris diomedea*
☐ Pink-footed Shearwater *Puffinus creatopus*
☐ Flesh-footed Shearwater *Puffinus carneipes*
☐ Greater Shearwater *Puffinus gravis*
☐ Wedge-tailed Shearwater *Puffinus pacificus*
☐ Buller's Shearwater *Puffinus bulleri*
☐ Sooty Shearwater *Puffinus griseus*
☐ Short-tailed Shearwater *Puffinus tenuirostris*

- ☐ Manx Shearwater *Puffinus puffinus*
- ☐ Black-vented Shearwater *Puffinus opisthomelas*
- ☐ Audubon's Shearwater *Puffinus lherminieri*
- ☐ Little Shearwater *Puffinus assimilis*

HYDROBATIDAE

- ☐ Wilson's Storm-Petrel *Oceanites oceanicus*
- ☐ White-faced Storm-Petrel *Pelagodroma marina*
- ☐ European Storm-Petrel *Hydrobates pelagicus*
- ☐ Fork-tailed Storm-Petrel *Oceanodroma furcata*
- ☐ Leach's Storm-Petrel *Oceanodroma leucorhoa*
- ☐ Ashy Storm-Petrel *Oceanodroma homochroa*
- ☐ Band-rumped Storm-Petrel *Oceanodroma castro*
- ☐ Wedge-rumped Storm-Petrel *Oceanodroma tethys*
- ☐ Black Storm-Petrel *Oceanodroma melania*
- ☐ Least Storm-Petrel *Oceanodroma microsoma*

PELECANIFORMES

PHAETHONTIDAE

- ☐ White-tailed Tropicbird *Phaethon lepturus*
- ☐ Red-billed Tropicbird *Phaethon aethereus*
- ☐ Red-tailed Tropicbird *Phaethon rubricauda*

SULIDAE

- ☐ Masked Booby *Sula dactylatra*
- ☐ Blue-footed Booby *Sula nebouxii*
- ☐ Brown Booby *Sula leucogaster*
- ☐ Red-footed Booby *Sula sula*
- ☐ Northern Gannet *Morus bassanus*

PELECANIDAE

- ☐ American White Pelican *Pelecanus erythrorhynchos*
- ☐ Brown Pelican *Pelecanus occidentalis*

PHALACROCORACIDAE

- ☐ Brandt's Cormorant *Phalacrocorax penicillatus*

- ☐ Neotropic Cormorant *Phalacrocorax brasilianus*
- ☐ Double-crested Cormorant *Phalacrocorax auritus*
- ☐ Great Cormorant *Phalacrocorax carbo*
- ☐ Red-faced Cormorant *Phalacrocorax urile*
- ☐ Pelagic Cormorant *Phalacrocorax pelagicus*

ANHINGIDAE

- ☐ Anhinga *Anhinga anhinga*

FREGATIDAE

- ☐ Magnificent Frigatebird *Fregata magnificens*
- ☐ Great Frigatebird *Fregata minor*
- ☐ Lesser Frigatebird *Fregata ariel*

CICONIIFORMES

ARDEIDAE

- ☐ American Bittern *Botaurus lentiginosus*
- ☐ Yellow Bittern *Ixobrychus sinensis*
- ☐ Least Bittern *Ixobrychus exilis*
- ☐ Great Blue Heron *Ardea herodias*
- ☐ Great Egret *Ardea alba*
- ☐ Chinese Egret *Egretta eulophotes*
- ☐ Little Egret *Egretta garzetta*
- ☐ Western Reef-Heron *Egretta gularis*
- ☐ Snowy Egret *Egretta thula*
- ☐ Little Blue Heron *Egretta caerulea*
- ☐ Tricolored Heron *Egretta tricolor*
- ☐ Reddish Egret *Egretta rufescens*
- ☐ Cattle Egret *Bubulcus ibis*
- ☐ Green Heron *Butorides virescens*
- ☐ Black-crowned Night-Heron *Nycticorax nycticorax*
- ☐ Yellow-crowned Night-Heron *Nyctanassa violacea*

THRESKIORNITHIDAE

- ☐ White Ibis *Eudocimus albus*
- ☐ Scarlet Ibis *Eudocimus ruber*
- ☐ Glossy Ibis *Plegadis falcinellus*
- ☐ White-faced Ibis *Plegadis chihi*
- ☐ Roseate Spoonbill *Ajaia ajaja*

CICONIIDAE

- ☐ Jabiru *Jabiru mycteria*
- ☐ Wood Stork *Mycteria americana*

CATHARTIDAE

☐ Black Vulture *Coragyps atratus*
☐ Turkey Vulture *Cathartes aura*
☐ California Condor *Gymnogyps californianus*

PHOENICOPTERIFORMES

PHOENICOPTERIDAE

☐ Greater Flamingo *Phoenicopterus ruber*

ANSERIFORMES

ANATIDAE

☐ Black-bellied Whistling-Duck *Dendrocygna autumnalis*
☐ Fulvous Whistling-Duck *Dendrocygna bicolor*
☐ Bean Goose *Anser fabalis*
☐ Pink-footed Goose *Anser brachyrhynchus*
☐ Greater White-fronted Goose *Anser albifrons*
☐ Lesser White-fronted Goose *Anser erythropus*
☐ Emperor Goose *Chen canagica*
☐ Snow Goose *Chen caerulescens*
☐ Ross's Goose *Chen rossii*
☐ Canada Goose *Branta canadensis*
☐ Brant *Branta bernicla*
☐ Barnacle Goose *Branta leucopsis*
☐ Mute Swan *Cygnus olor*
☐ Trumpeter Swan *Cygnus buccinator*
☐ Tundra Swan *Cygnus columbianus*
☐ Whooper Swan *Cygnus cygnus*
☐ Muscovy Duck *Cairina moschata*
☐ Wood Duck *Aix sponsa*
☐ Gadwall *Anas strepera*
☐ Falcated Duck *Anas falcata*
☐ Eurasian Wigeon *Anas penelope*
☐ American Wigeon *Anas americana*
☐ American Black Duck *Anas rubripes*
☐ Mallard *Anas platyrhynchos*
☐ Mottled Duck *Anas fulvigula*
☐ Spot-billed Duck *Anas poecilorhyncha*
☐ Blue-winged Teal *Anas discors*
☐ Cinnamon Teal *Anas cyanoptera*
☐ Northern Shoveler *Anas clypeata*
☐ White-cheeked Pintail *Anas bahamensis*
☐ Northern Pintail *Anas acuta*
☐ Garganey *Anas querquedula*
☐ Baikal Teal *Anas formosa*
☐ Green-winged Teal *Anas crecca*

☐ Canvasback *Aythya valisineria*
☐ Redhead *Aythya americana*
☐ Common Pochard *Aythya ferina*
☐ Ring-necked Duck *Aythya collaris*
☐ Tufted Duck *Aythya fuligula*
☐ Greater Scaup *Aythya marila*
☐ Lesser Scaup *Aythya affinis*
☐ Steller's Eider *Polysticta stelleri*
☐ Spectacled Eider *Somateria fischeri*
☐ King Eider *Somateria spectabilis*
☐ Common Eider *Somateria mollissima*
☐ Harlequin Duck *Histrionicus histrionicus*
☐ Surf Scoter *Melanitta perspicillata*
☐ White-winged Scoter *Melanitta fusca*
☐ Black Scoter *Melanitta nigra*
☐ Oldsquaw *Clangula hyemalis*
☐ Bufflehead *Bucephala albeola*
☐ Common Goldeneye *Bucephala clangula*
☐ Barrow's Goldeneye *Bucephala islandica*
☐ Smew *Mergellus albellus*
☐ Hooded Merganser *Lophodytes cucullatus*
☐ Common Merganser *Mergus merganser*
☐ Red-breasted Merganser *Mergus serrator*
☐ Masked Duck *Nomonyx dominicus*
☐ Ruddy Duck *Oxyura jamaicensis*

FALCONIFORMES

ACCIPITRIDAE

☐ Osprey *Pandion haliaetus*
☐ Hook-billed Kite *Chondrohierax uncinatus*
☐ Swallow-tailed Kite *Elanoides forficatus*
☐ White-tailed Kite *Elanus leucurus*
☐ Snail Kite *Rostrhamus sociabilis*
☐ Mississippi Kite *Ictinia mississippiensis*
☐ Bald Eagle *Haliaeetus leucocephalus*
☐ White-tailed Eagle *Haliaeetus albicilla*
☐ Steller's Sea-Eagle *Haliaeetus pelagicus*
☐ Northern Harrier *Circus cyaneus*
☐ Sharp-shinned Hawk *Accipiter striatus*
☐ Cooper's Hawk *Accipiter cooperii*
☐ Northern Goshawk *Accipiter gentilis*
☐ Crane Hawk *Geranospiza caerulescens*
☐ Gray Hawk *Asturina nitida*
☐ Common Black-Hawk *Buteogallus anthracinus*
☐ Harris's Hawk *Parabuteo unicinctus*

- [ ] Roadside Hawk *Buteo magnirostris*
- [ ] Red-shouldered Hawk *Buteo lineatus*
- [ ] Broad-winged Hawk *Buteo platypterus*
- [ ] Short-tailed Hawk *Buteo brachyurus*
- [ ] Swainson's Hawk *Buteo swainsoni*
- [ ] White-tailed Hawk *Buteo albicaudatus*
- [ ] Zone-tailed Hawk *Buteo albonotatus*
- [ ] Red-tailed Hawk *Buteo jamaicensis*
- [ ] Ferruginous Hawk *Buteo regalis*
- [ ] Rough-legged Hawk *Buteo lagopus*
- [ ] Golden Eagle *Aquila chrysaetos*

FALCONIDAE

- [ ] Collared Forest-Falcon *Micrastur semitorquatus*
- [ ] Crested Caracara *Caracara plancus*
- [ ] Eurasian Kestrel *Falco tinnunculus*
- [ ] American Kestrel *Falco sparverius*
- [ ] Merlin *Falco columbarius*
- [ ] Eurasian Hobby *Falco subbuteo*
- [ ] Aplomado Falcon *Falco femoralis*
- [ ] Gyrfalcon *Falco rusticolus*
- [ ] Peregrine Falcon *Falco peregrinus*
- [ ] Prairie Falcon *Falco mexicanus*

GALLIFORMES

CRACIDAE

- [ ] Plain Chachalaca *Ortalis vetula*

PHASIANIDAE

- [ ] Chukar *Alectoris chukar*
- [ ] Himalayan Snowcock *Tetraogallus himalayensis*
- [ ] Gray Partridge *Perdix perdix*
- [ ] Ring-necked Pheasant *Phasianus colchicus*
- [ ] Ruffed Grouse *Bonasa umbellus*
- [ ] Sage Grouse *Centrocercus urophasianus*
- [ ] Spruce Grouse *Falcipennis canadensis*
- [ ] Willow Ptarmigan *Lagopus lagopus*
- [ ] Rock Ptarmigan *Lagopus mutus*
- [ ] White-tailed Ptarmigan *Lagopus leucurus*
- [ ] Blue Grouse *Dendragapus obscurus*
- [ ] Sharp-tailed Grouse *Tympanuchus phasianellus*
- [ ] Greater Prairie-Chicken *Tympanuchus cupido*
- [ ] Lesser Prairie-Chicken *Tympanuchus pallidicinctus*
- [ ] Wild Turkey *Meleagris gallopavo*

ODONTOPHORIDAE

- [ ] Mountain Quail *Oreortyx pictus*
- [ ] Scaled Quail *Callipepla squamata*
- [ ] Elegant Quail *Callipepla douglasii*
- [ ] California Quail *Callipepla californica*
- [ ] Gambel's Quail *Callipepla gambelii*
- [ ] Northern Bobwhite *Colinus virginianus*
- [ ] Montezuma Quail *Cyrtonyx montezumae*

GRUIFORMES

RALLIDAE

- [ ] Yellow Rail *Coturnicops noveboracensis*
- [ ] Black Rail *Laterallus jamaicensis*
- [ ] Corn Crake *Crex crex*
- [ ] Clapper Rail *Rallus longirostris*
- [ ] King Rail *Rallus elegans*
- [ ] Virginia Rail *Rallus limicola*
- [ ] Sora *Porzana carolina*
- [ ] Paint-billed Crake *Neocrex erythrops*
- [ ] Spotted Rail *Pardirallus maculatus*
- [ ] Purple Gallinule *Porphyrula martinica*
- [ ] Azure Gallinule *Porphyrula flavirostris*
- [ ] Common Moorhen *Gallinula chloropus*
- [ ] Eurasian Coot *Fulica atra*
- [ ] American Coot *Fulica americana*

ARAMIDAE

- [ ] Limpkin *Aramus guarauna*

GRUIDAE

- [ ] Sandhill Crane *Grus canadensis*
- [ ] Common Crane *Grus grus*
- [ ] Whooping Crane *Grus americana*

CHARADRIIFORMES

BURHINIDAE

- [ ] Double-striped Thick-knee *Burhinus bistriatus*

CHARADRIIDAE

- [ ] Northern Lapwing *Vanellus vanellus*
- [ ] Black-bellied Plover *Pluvialis squatarola*
- [ ] European Golden-Plover *Pluvialis apricaria*
- [ ] American Golden-Plover *Pluvialis dominica*
- [ ] Pacific Golden-Plover *Pluvialis fulva*

☐ Mongolian Plover *Charadrius mongolus*
☐ Collared Plover *Charadrius collaris*
☐ Snowy Plover *Charadrius alexandrinus*
☐ Wilson's Plover *Charadrius wilsonia*
☐ Common Ringed Plover *Charadrius hiaticula*
☐ Semipalmated Plover *Charadrius semipalmatus*
☐ Piping Plover *Charadrius melodus*
☐ Little Ringed Plover *Charadrius dubius*
☐ Killdeer *Charadrius vociferus*
☐ Mountain Plover *Charadrius montanus*
☐ Eurasian Dotterel *Charadrius morinellus*

HAEMATOPODIDAE

☐ Eurasian Oystercatcher *Haematopus ostralegus*
☐ American Oystercatcher *Haematopus palliatus*
☐ Black Oystercatcher *Haematopus bachmani*

RECURVIROSTRIDAE

☐ Black-winged Stilt *Himantopus himantopus*
☐ Black-necked Stilt *Himantopus mexicanus*
☐ American Avocet *Recurvirostra americana*

JACANIDAE

☐ Northern Jacana *Jacana spinosa*

SCOLOPACIDAE

☐ Common Greenshank *Tringa nebularia*
☐ Greater Yellowlegs *Tringa melanoleuca*
☐ Lesser Yellowlegs *Tringa flavipes*
☐ Marsh Sandpiper *Tringa stagnatilis*
☐ Common Redshank *Tringa totanus*
☐ Spotted Redshank *Tringa erythropus*
☐ Wood Sandpiper *Tringa glareola*
☐ Green Sandpiper *Tringa ochropus*
☐ Solitary Sandpiper *Tringa solitaria*
☐ Willet *Catoptrophorus semipalmatus*
☐ Wandering Tattler *Heteroscelus incanus*
☐ Gray-tailed Tattler *Heteroscelus brevipes*

☐ Common Sandpiper *Actitis hypoleucos*
☐ Spotted Sandpiper *Actitis macularia*
☐ Terek Sandpiper *Xenus cinereus*
☐ Upland Sandpiper *Bartramia longicauda*
☐ Little Curlew *Numenius minutus*
☐ Eskimo Curlew *Numenius borealis*
☐ Whimbrel *Numenius phaeopus*
☐ Bristle-thighed Curlew *Numenius tahitiensis*
☐ Far Eastern Curlew *Numenius madagascariensis*
☐ Slender-billed Curlew *Numenius tenuirostris*
☐ Eurasian Curlew *Numenius arquata*
☐ Long-billed Curlew *Numenius americanus*
☐ Black-tailed Godwit *Limosa limosa*
☐ Hudsonian Godwit *Limosa haemastica*
☐ Bar-tailed Godwit *Limosa lapponica*
☐ Marbled Godwit *Limosa fedoa*
☐ Ruddy Turnstone *Arenaria interpres*
☐ Black Turnstone *Arenaria melanocephala*
☐ Surfbird *Aphriza virgata*
☐ Great Knot *Calidris tenuirostris*
☐ Red Knot *Calidris canutus*
☐ Sanderling *Calidris alba*
☐ Semipalmated Sandpiper *Calidris pusilla*
☐ Western Sandpiper *Calidris mauri*
☐ Red-necked Stint *Calidris ruficollis*
☐ Little Stint *Calidris minuta*
☐ Temminck's Stint *Calidris temminckii*
☐ Long-toed Stint *Calidris subminuta*
☐ Least Sandpiper *Calidris minutilla*
☐ White-rumped Sandpiper *Calidris fuscicollis*
☐ Baird's Sandpiper *Calidris bairdii*
☐ Pectoral Sandpiper *Calidris melanotos*
☐ Sharp-tailed Sandpiper *Calidris acuminata*
☐ Purple Sandpiper *Calidris maritima*
☐ Rock Sandpiper *Calidris ptilocnemis*
☐ Dunlin *Calidris alpina*
☐ Curlew Sandpiper *Calidris ferruginea*
☐ Stilt Sandpiper *Calidris himantopus*
☐ Spoonbill Sandpiper *Eurynorhynchus pygmeus*
☐ Broad-billed Sandpiper *Limicola falcinellus*
☐ Buff-breasted Sandpiper *Tryngites subruficollis*
☐ Ruff *Philomachus pugnax*

- ☐ Short-billed Dowitcher *Limnodromus griseus*
- ☐ Long-billed Dowitcher *Limnodromus scolopaceus*
- ☐ Jack Snipe *Lymnocryptes minimus*
- ☐ Common Snipe *Gallinago gallinago*
- ☐ Pin-tailed Snipe *Gallinago stenura*
- ☐ Eurasian Woodcock *Scolopax rusticola*
- ☐ American Woodcock *Scolopax minor*
- ☐ Wilson's Phalarope *Phalaropus tricolor*
- ☐ Red-necked Phalarope *Phalaropus lobatus*
- ☐ Red Phalarope *Phalaropus fulicaria*

GLAREOLIDAE

- ☐ Oriental Pratincole *Glareola maldivarum*

LARIDAE

- ☐ Great Skua *Catharacta skua*
- ☐ South Polar Skua *Catharacta maccormicki*
- ☐ Pomarine Jaeger *Stercorarius pomarinus*
- ☐ Parasitic Jaeger *Stercorarius parasiticus*
- ☐ Long-tailed Jaeger *Stercorarius longicaudus*
- ☐ Laughing Gull *Larus atricilla*
- ☐ Franklin's Gull *Larus pipixcan*
- ☐ Little Gull *Larus minutus*
- ☐ Black-headed Gull *Larus ridibundus*
- ☐ Bonaparte's Gull *Larus philadelphia*
- ☐ Heermann's Gull *Larus heermanni*
- ☐ Band-tailed Gull *Larus belcheri*
- ☐ Black-tailed Gull *Larus crassirostris*
- ☐ Mew Gull *Larus canus*
- ☐ Ring-billed Gull *Larus delawarensis*
- ☐ California Gull *Larus californicus*
- ☐ Herring Gull *Larus argentatus*
- ☐ Yellow-legged Gull *Larus cachinnans*
- ☐ Thayer's Gull *Larus thayeri*
- ☐ Iceland Gull *Larus glaucoides*
- ☐ Lesser Black-backed Gull *Larus fuscus*
- ☐ Slaty-backed Gull *Larus schistisagus*
- ☐ Yellow-footed Gull *Larus livens*
- ☐ Western Gull *Larus occidentalis*
- ☐ Glaucous-winged Gull *Larus glaucescens*
- ☐ Glaucous Gull *Larus hyperboreus*
- ☐ Great Black-backed Gull *Larus marinus*
- ☐ Sabine's Gull *Xema sabini*
- ☐ Black-legged Kittiwake *Rissa tridactyla*
- ☐ Red-legged Kittiwake *Rissa brevirostris*
- ☐ Ross's Gull *Rhodostethia rosea*

- ☐ Ivory Gull *Pagophila eburnea*
- ☐ Gull-billed Tern *Sterna nilotica*
- ☐ Caspian Tern *Sterna caspia*
- ☐ Royal Tern *Sterna maxima*
- ☐ Elegant Tern *Sterna elegans*
- ☐ Sandwich Tern *Sterna sandvicensis*
- ☐ Roseate Tern *Sterna dougallii*
- ☐ Common Tern *Sterna hirundo*
- ☐ Arctic Tern *Sterna paradisaea*
- ☐ Forster's Tern *Sterna forsteri*
- ☐ Least Tern *Sterna antillarum*
- ☐ Aleutian Tern *Sterna aleutica*
- ☐ Bridled Tern *Sterna anaethetus*
- ☐ Sooty Tern *Sterna fuscata*
- ☐ Large-billed Tern *Phaetusa simplex*
- ☐ White-winged Tern *Chlidonias leucopterus*
- ☐ Whiskered Tern *Chlidonias hybridus*
- ☐ Black Tern *Chlidonias niger*
- ☐ Brown Noddy *Anous stolidus*
- ☐ Black Noddy *Anous minutus*
- ☐ Black Skimmer *Rynchops niger*

ALCIDAE

- ☐ Dovekie *Alle alle*
- ☐ Common Murre *Uria aalge*
- ☐ Thick-billed Murre *Uria lomvia*
- ☐ Razorbill *Alca torda*
- ☐ Black Guillemot *Cepphus grylle*
- ☐ Pigeon Guillemot *Cepphus columba*
- ☐ Long-billed Murrelet *Brachyramphus perdix*
- ☐ Marbled Murrelet *Brachyramphus marmoratus*
- ☐ Kittlitz's Murrelet *Brachyramphus brevirostris*
- ☐ Xantus's Murrelet *Synthliboramphus hypoleucus*
- ☐ Craveri's Murrelet *Synthliboramphus craveri*
- ☐ Ancient Murrelet *Synthliboramphus antiquus*
- ☐ Cassin's Auklet *Ptychoramphus aleuticus*
- ☐ Parakeet Auklet *Aethia psittacula*
- ☐ Least Auklet *Aethia pusilla*
- ☐ Whiskered Auklet *Aethia pygmaea*
- ☐ Crested Auklet *Aethia cristatella*
- ☐ Rhinoceros Auklet *Cerorhinca monocerata*
- ☐ Atlantic Puffin *Fratercula arctica*
- ☐ Horned Puffin *Fratercula corniculata*
- ☐ Tufted Puffin *Fratercula cirrhata*

COLUMBIFORMES

COLUMBIDAE

- [ ] Rock Dove *Columba livia*
- [ ] Scaly-naped Pigeon *Columba squamosa*
- [ ] White-crowned Pigeon *Columba leucocephala*
- [ ] Red-billed Pigeon *Columba flavirostris*
- [ ] Band-tailed Pigeon *Columba fasciata*
- [ ] Oriental Turtle-Dove *Streptopelia orientalis*
- [ ] Eurasian Collared-Dove *Streptopelia decaocto*
- [ ] Spotted Dove *Streptopelia chinensis*
- [ ] White-winged Dove *Zenaida asiatica*
- [ ] Zenaida Dove *Zenaida aurita*
- [ ] Mourning Dove *Zenaida macroura*
- [ ] Inca Dove *Columbina inca*
- [ ] Common Ground-Dove *Columbina passerina*
- [ ] Ruddy Ground-Dove *Columbina talpacoti*
- [ ] White-tipped Dove *Leptotila verreauxi*
- [ ] Key West Quail-Dove *Geotrygon chrysia*
- [ ] Ruddy Quail-Dove *Geotrygon montana*

PSITTACIFORMES

PSITTACIDAE

- [ ] Budgerigar *Melopsittacus undulatus*
- [ ] Monk Parakeet *Myiopsitta monachus*
- [ ] Thick-billed Parrot *Rhynchopsitta pachyrhyncha*
- [ ] White-winged Parakeet *Brotogeris versicolurus*
- [ ] Red-crowned Parrot *Amazona viridigenalis*

CUCULIFORMES

CUCULIDAE

- [ ] Common Cuckoo *Cuculus canorus*
- [ ] Oriental Cuckoo *Cuculus saturatus*
- [ ] Black-billed Cuckoo *Coccyzus erythropthalmus*
- [ ] Yellow-billed Cuckoo *Coccyzus americanus*
- [ ] Mangrove Cuckoo *Coccyzus minor*
- [ ] Greater Roadrunner *Geococcyx californianus*
- [ ] Smooth-billed Ani *Crotophaga ani*
- [ ] Groove-billed Ani *Crotophaga sulcirostris*

STRIGIFORMES

TYTONIDAE

- [ ] Barn Owl *Tyto alba*

STRIGIDAE

- [ ] Flammulated Owl *Otus flammeolus*
- [ ] Oriental Scops-Owl *Otus sunia*
- [ ] Western Screech-Owl *Otus kennicottii*
- [ ] Eastern Screech-Owl *Otus asio*
- [ ] Whiskered Screech-Owl *Otus trichopsis*
- [ ] Great Horned Owl *Bubo virginianus*
- [ ] Snowy Owl *Nyctea scandiaca*
- [ ] Northern Hawk Owl *Surnia ulula*
- [ ] Northern Pygmy-Owl *Glaucidium gnoma*
- [ ] Ferruginous Pygmy-Owl *Glaucidium brasilianum*
- [ ] Elf Owl *Micrathene whitneyi*
- [ ] Burrowing Owl *Athene cunicularia*
- [ ] Mottled Owl *Ciccaba virgata*
- [ ] Spotted Owl *Strix occidentalis*
- [ ] Barred Owl *Strix varia*
- [ ] Great Gray Owl *Strix nebulosa*
- [ ] Long-eared Owl *Asio otus*
- [ ] Stygian Owl *Asio stygius*
- [ ] Short-eared Owl *Asio flammeus*
- [ ] Boreal Owl *Aegolius funereus*
- [ ] Northern Saw-whet Owl *Aegolius acadicus*

CAPRIMULGIFORMES

CAPRIMULGIDAE

- [ ] Lesser Nighthawk *Chordeiles acutipennis*
- [ ] Common Nighthawk *Chordeiles minor*
- [ ] Antillean Nighthawk *Chordeiles gundlachii*
- [ ] Common Pauraque *Nyctidromus albicollis*
- [ ] Common Poorwill *Phalaenoptilus nuttallii*
- [ ] Chuck-will's-widow *Caprimulgus carolinensis*
- [ ] Buff-collared Nightjar *Caprimulgus ridgwayi*
- [ ] Whip-poor-will *Caprimulgus vociferus*
- [ ] Jungle Nightjar *Caprimulgus indicus*

APODIFORMES

APODIDAE

- ☐ Black Swift *Cypseloides niger*
- ☐ White-collared Swift *Streptoprocne zonaris*
- ☐ Chimney Swift *Chaetura pelagica*
- ☐ Vaux's Swift *Chaetura vauxi*
- ☐ White-throated Needletail *Hirundapus caudacutus*
- ☐ Common Swift *Apus apus*
- ☐ Fork-tailed Swift *Apus pacificus*
- ☐ White-throated Swift *Aeronautes saxatalis*
- ☐ Antillean Palm-Swift *Tachornis phoenicobia*

TROCHILIDAE

- ☐ Green Violet-ear *Colibri thalassinus*
- ☐ Green-breasted Mango *Anthracothorax prevostii*
- ☐ Broad-billed Hummingbird *Cynanthus latirostris*
- ☐ White-eared Hummingbird *Hylocharis leucotis*
- ☐ Xantus's Hummingbird *Hylocharis xantusii*
- ☐ Berylline Hummingbird *Amazilia beryllina*
- ☐ Buff-bellied Hummingbird *Amazilia yucatanensis*
- ☐ Cinnamon Hummingbird *Amazilia rutila*
- ☐ Violet-crowned Hummingbird *Amazilia violiceps*
- ☐ Blue-throated Hummingbird *Lampornis clemenciae*
- ☐ Magnificent Hummingbird *Eugenes fulgens*
- ☐ Plain-capped Starthroat *Heliomaster constantii*
- ☐ Bahama Woodstar *Calliphlox evelynae*
- ☐ Lucifer Hummingbird *Calothorax lucifer*
- ☐ Ruby-throated Hummingbird *Archilochus colubris*
- ☐ Black-chinned Hummingbird *Archilochus alexandri*
- ☐ Anna's Hummingbird *Calypte anna*
- ☐ Costa's Hummingbird *Calypte costae*
- ☐ Calliope Hummingbird *Stellula calliope*
- ☐ Bumblebee Hummingbird *Atthis heloisa*
- ☐ Broad-tailed Hummingbird *Selasphorus platycercus*
- ☐ Rufous Hummingbird *Selasphorus rufus*
- ☐ Allen's Hummingbird *Selasphorus sasin*

TROGONIFORMES

TROGONIDAE

- ☐ Elegant Trogon *Trogon elegans*
- ☐ Eared Trogon *Euptilotis neoxenus*

UPUPIFORMES

UPUPIDAE

- ☐ Eurasian Hoopoe *Upupa epops*

CORACIIFORMES

ALCEDINIDAE

- ☐ Ringed Kingfisher *Ceryle torquata*
- ☐ Belted Kingfisher *Ceryle alcyon*
- ☐ Green Kingfisher *Chloroceryle americana*

PICIFORMES

PICIDAE

- ☐ Eurasian Wryneck *Jynx torquilla*
- ☐ Lewis's Woodpecker *Melanerpes lewis*
- ☐ Red-headed Woodpecker *Melanerpes erythrocephalus*
- ☐ Acorn Woodpecker *Melanerpes formicivorus*
- ☐ Gila Woodpecker *Melanerpes uropygialis*
- ☐ Golden-fronted Woodpecker *Melanerpes aurifrons*
- ☐ Red-bellied Woodpecker *Melanerpes carolinus*
- ☐ Williamson's Sapsucker *Sphyrapicus thyroideus*
- ☐ Yellow-bellied Sapsucker *Sphyrapicus varius*
- ☐ Red-naped Sapsucker *Sphyrapicus nuchalis*
- ☐ Red-breasted Sapsucker *Sphyrapicus ruber*
- ☐ Great Spotted Woodpecker *Dendrocopos major*
- ☐ Ladder-backed Woodpecker *Picoides scalaris*
- ☐ Nuttall's Woodpecker *Picoides nuttallii*
- ☐ Downy Woodpecker *Picoides pubescens*

☐ Hairy Woodpecker *Picoides villosus*
☐ Strickland's Woodpecker *Picoides stricklandi*
☐ Red-cockaded Woodpecker *Picoides borealis*
☐ White-headed Woodpecker *Picoides albolarvatus*
☐ Three-toed Woodpecker *Picoides tridactylus*
☐ Black-backed Woodpecker *Picoides arcticus*
☐ Northern Flicker *Colaptes auratus*
☐ Gilded Flicker *Colaptes chrysoides*
☐ Pileated Woodpecker *Dryocopus pileatus*
☐ Ivory-billed Woodpecker *Campephilus principalis*

PASSERIFORMES

TYRANNIDAE

☐ Northern Beardless-Tyrannulet *Camptostoma imberbe*
☐ Greenish Elaenia *Myiopagis viridicata*
☐ Caribbean Elaenia *Elaenia martinica*
☐ Tufted Flycatcher *Mitrephanes phaeocercus*
☐ Olive-sided Flycatcher *Contopus cooperi*
☐ Greater Pewee *Contopus pertinax*
☐ Western Wood-Pewee *Contopus sordidulus*
☐ Eastern Wood-Pewee *Contopus virens*
☐ Cuban Pewee *Contopus caribaeus*
☐ Yellow-bellied Flycatcher *Empidonax flaviventris*
☐ Acadian Flycatcher *Empidonax virescens*
☐ Alder Flycatcher *Empidonax alnorum*
☐ Willow Flycatcher *Empidonax traillii*
☐ Least Flycatcher *Empidonax minimus*
☐ Hammond's Flycatcher *Empidonax hammondii*
☐ Gray Flycatcher *Empidonax wrightii*
☐ Dusky Flycatcher *Empidonax oberholseri*
☐ Pacific-slope Flycatcher *Empidonax difficilis*
☐ Cordilleran Flycatcher *Empidonax occidentalis*
☐ Buff-breasted Flycatcher *Empidonax fulvifrons*
☐ Black Phoebe *Sayornis nigricans*
☐ Eastern Phoebe *Sayornis phoebe*
☐ Say's Phoebe *Sayornis saya*

☐ Vermilion Flycatcher *Pyrocephalus rubinus*
☐ Dusky-capped Flycatcher *Myiarchus tuberculifer*
☐ Ash-throated Flycatcher *Myiarchus cinerascens*
☐ Nutting's Flycatcher *Myiarchus nuttingi*
☐ Great Crested Flycatcher *Myiarchus crinitus*
☐ Brown-crested Flycatcher *Myiarchus tyrannulus*
☐ La Sagra's Flycatcher *Myiarchus sagrae*
☐ Great Kiskadee *Pitangus sulphuratus*
☐ Sulphur-bellied Flycatcher *Myiodynastes luteiventris*
☐ Piratic Flycatcher *Legatus leucophaius*
☐ Variegated Flycatcher *Empidonomus varius*
☐ Tropical Kingbird *Tyrannus melancholicus*
☐ Couch's Kingbird *Tyrannus couchii*
☐ Cassin's Kingbird *Tyrannus vociferans*
☐ Thick-billed Kingbird *Tyrannus crassirostris*
☐ Western Kingbird *Tyrannus verticalis*
☐ Eastern Kingbird *Tyrannus tyrannus*
☐ Gray Kingbird *Tyrannus dominicensis*
☐ Loggerhead Kingbird *Tyrannus caudifasciatus*
☐ Scissor-tailed Flycatcher *Tyrannus forficatus*
☐ Fork-tailed Flycatcher *Tyrannus savana*
☐ Rose-throated Becard *Pachyramphus aglaiae*
☐ Masked Tityra *Tityra semifasciata*

LANIIDAE

☐ Brown Shrike *Lanius cristatus*
☐ Loggerhead Shrike *Lanius ludovicianus*
☐ Northern Shrike *Lanius excubitor*

VIREONIDAE

☐ White-eyed Vireo *Vireo griseus*
☐ Thick-billed Vireo *Vireo crassirostris*
☐ Bell's Vireo *Vireo bellii*
☐ Black-capped Vireo *Vireo atricapillus*
☐ Gray Vireo *Vireo vicinior*
☐ Yellow-throated Vireo *Vireo flavifrons*
☐ Plumbeous Vireo *Vireo plumbeus*
☐ Cassin's Vireo *Vireo cassinii*
☐ Blue-headed Vireo *Vireo solitarius*
☐ Hutton's Vireo *Vireo huttoni*

- ☐ Warbling Vireo *Vireo gilvus*
- ☐ Philadelphia Vireo *Vireo philadelphicus*
- ☐ Red-eyed Vireo *Vireo olivaceus*
- ☐ Yellow-green Vireo *Vireo flavoviridis*
- ☐ Black-whiskered Vireo *Vireo altiloquus*
- ☐ Yucatan Vireo *Vireo magister*

CORVIDAE

- ☐ Gray Jay *Perisoreus canadensis*
- ☐ Steller's Jay *Cyanocitta stelleri*
- ☐ Blue Jay *Cyanocitta cristata*
- ☐ Green Jay *Cyanocorax yncas*
- ☐ Brown Jay *Cyanocorax morio*
- ☐ Florida Scrub-Jay *Aphelocoma coerulescens*
- ☐ Island Scrub-Jay *Aphelocoma insularis*
- ☐ Western Scrub-Jay *Aphelocoma californica*
- ☐ Mexican Jay *Aphelocoma ultramarina*
- ☐ Pinyon Jay *Gymnorhinus cyanocephalus*
- ☐ Clark's Nutcracker *Nucifraga columbiana*
- ☐ Black-billed Magpie *Pica pica*
- ☐ Yellow-billed Magpie *Pica nuttalli*
- ☐ Eurasian Jackdaw *Corvus monedula*
- ☐ American Crow *Corvus brachyrhynchos*
- ☐ Northwestern Crow *Corvus caurinus*
- ☐ Tamaulipas Crow *Corvus imparatus*
- ☐ Fish Crow *Corvus ossifragus*
- ☐ Chihuahuan Raven *Corvus cryptoleucus*
- ☐ Common Raven *Corvus corax*

ALAUDIDAE

- ☐ Sky Lark *Alauda arvensis*
- ☐ Horned Lark *Eremophila alpestris*

HIRUNDINIDAE

- ☐ Purple Martin *Progne subis*
- ☐ Cuban Martin *Progne cryptoleuca*
- ☐ Caribbean Martin *Progne dominicensis*
- ☐ Gray-breasted Martin *Progne chalybea*
- ☐ Southern Martin *Progne elegans*
- ☐ Brown-chested Martin *Progne tapera*
- ☐ Tree Swallow *Tachycineta bicolor*
- ☐ Violet-green Swallow *Tachycineta thalassina*
- ☐ Bahama Swallow *Tachycineta cyaneoviridis*

- ☐ Northern Rough-winged Swallow *Stelgidopteryx serripennis*
- ☐ Bank Swallow *Riparia riparia*
- ☐ Cliff Swallow *Petrochelidon pyrrhonota*
- ☐ Cave Swallow *Petrochelidon fulva*
- ☐ Barn Swallow *Hirundo rustica*
- ☐ Common House-Martin *Delichon urbica*

PARIDAE

- ☐ Carolina Chickadee *Poecile carolinensis*
- ☐ Black-capped Chickadee *Poecile atricapillus*
- ☐ Mountain Chickadee *Poecile gambeli*
- ☐ Mexican Chickadee *Poecile sclateri*
- ☐ Chestnut-backed Chickadee *Poecile rufescens*
- ☐ Boreal Chickadee *Poecile hudsonicus*
- ☐ Gray-headed Chickadee *Poecile cinctus*
- ☐ Bridled Titmouse *Baeolophus wollweberi*
- ☐ Oak Titmouse *Baeolophus inornatus*
- ☐ Juniper Titmouse *Baeolophus griseus*
- ☐ Tufted Titmouse *Baeolophus bicolor*

REMIZIDAE

- ☐ Verdin *Auriparus flaviceps*

AEGITHALIDAE

- ☐ Bushtit *Psaltriparus minimus*

SITTIDAE

- ☐ Red-breasted Nuthatch *Sitta canadensis*
- ☐ White-breasted Nuthatch *Sitta carolinensis*
- ☐ Pygmy Nuthatch *Sitta pygmaea*
- ☐ Brown-headed Nuthatch *Sitta pusilla*

CERTHIIDAE

- ☐ Brown Creeper *Certhia americana*

TROGLODYTIDAE

- ☐ Cactus Wren *Campylorhynchus brunneicapillus*
- ☐ Rock Wren *Salpinctes obsoletus*
- ☐ Canyon Wren *Catherpes mexicanus*
- ☐ Carolina Wren *Thryothorus ludovicianus*
- ☐ Bewick's Wren *Thryomanes bewickii*

☐ House Wren *Troglodytes aedon*
☐ Winter Wren *Troglodytes troglodytes*
☐ Sedge Wren *Cistothorus platensis*
☐ Marsh Wren *Cistothorus palustris*

CINCLIDAE

☐ American Dipper *Cinclus mexicanus*

PYCNONOTIDAE

☐ Red-whiskered Bulbul *Pycnonotus jocosus*

REGULIDAE

☐ Golden-crowned Kinglet *Regulus satrapa*
☐ Ruby-crowned Kinglet *Regulus calendula*

SYLVIIDAE

☐ Middendorff's Grasshopper-Warbler *Locustella ochotensis*
☐ Lanceolated Warbler *Locustella lanceolata*
☐ Wood Warbler *Phylloscopus sibilatrix*
☐ Dusky Warbler *Phylloscopus fuscatus*
☐ Arctic Warbler *Phylloscopus borealis*
☐ Blue-gray Gnatcatcher *Polioptila caerulea*
☐ California Gnatcatcher *Polioptila californica*
☐ Black-tailed Gnatcatcher *Polioptila melanura*
☐ Black-capped Gnatcatcher *Polioptila nigriceps*

MUSCICAPIDAE

☐ Narcissus Flycatcher *Ficedula narcissina*
☐ Mugimaki Flycatcher *Ficedula mugimaki*
☐ Red-breasted Flycatcher *Ficedula parva*
☐ Siberian Flycatcher *Muscicapa sibirica*
☐ Gray-spotted Flycatcher *Muscicapa griseisticta*
☐ Asian Brown Flycatcher *Muscicapa dauurica*

TURDIDAE

☐ Siberian Rubythroat *Luscinia calliope*
☐ Bluethroat *Luscinia svecica*
☐ Siberian Blue Robin *Luscinia cyane*
☐ Red-flanked Bluetail *Tarsiger cyanurus*

☐ Northern Wheatear *Oenanthe oenanthe*
☐ Stonechat *Saxicola torquata*
☐ Eastern Bluebird *Sialia sialis*
☐ Western Bluebird *Sialia mexicana*
☐ Mountain Bluebird *Sialia currucoides*
☐ Townsend's Solitaire *Myadestes townsendi*
☐ Orange-billed Nightingale-Thrush *Catharus aurantiirostris*
☐ Veery *Catharus fuscescens*
☐ Gray-cheeked Thrush *Catharus minimus*
☐ Bicknell's Thrush *Catharus bicknelli*
☐ Swainson's Thrush *Catharus ustulatus*
☐ Hermit Thrush *Catharus guttatus*
☐ Wood Thrush *Hylocichla mustelina*
☐ Eurasian Blackbird *Turdus merula*
☐ Eyebrowed Thrush *Turdus obscurus*
☐ Dusky Thrush *Turdus naumanni*
☐ Fieldfare *Turdus pilaris*
☐ Redwing *Turdus iliacus*
☐ Clay-colored Robin *Turdus grayi*
☐ White-throated Robin *Turdus assimilis*
☐ Rufous-backed Robin *Turdus rufopalliatus*
☐ American Robin *Turdus migratorius*
☐ Varied Thrush *Ixoreus naevius*
☐ Aztec Thrush *Ridgwayia pinicola*

TIMALIIDAE

☐ Wrentit *Chamaea fasciata*

ZOSTEROPIDAE

☐ Japanese White-eye *Zosterops japonicus*

MIMIDAE

☐ Gray Catbird *Dumetella carolinensis*
☐ Northern Mockingbird *Mimus polyglottos*
☐ Bahama Mockingbird *Mimus gundlachii*
☐ Sage Thrasher *Oreoscoptes montanus*
☐ Brown Thrasher *Toxostoma rufum*
☐ Long-billed Thrasher *Toxostoma longirostre*
☐ Bendire's Thrasher *Toxostoma bendirei*
☐ Curve-billed Thrasher *Toxostoma curvirostre*
☐ California Thrasher *Toxostoma redivivum*
☐ Crissal Thrasher *Toxostoma crissale*

☐ Le Conte's Thrasher *Toxostoma lecontei*
☐ Blue Mockingbird *Melanotis caerulescens*

STURNIDAE

☐ European Starling *Sturnus vulgaris*
☐ Crested Myna *Acridotheres cristatellus*

PRUNELLIDAE

☐ Siberian Accentor *Prunella montanella*

MOTACILLIDAE

☐ Yellow Wagtail *Motacilla flava*
☐ Citrine Wagtail *Motacilla citreola*
☐ Gray Wagtail *Motacilla cinerea*
☐ White Wagtail *Motacilla alba*
☐ Black-backed Wagtail *Motacilla lugens*
☐ Tree Pipit *Anthus trivialis*
☐ Olive-backed Pipit *Anthus hodgsoni*
☐ Pechora Pipit *Anthus gustavi*
☐ Red-throated Pipit *Anthus cervinus*
☐ American Pipit *Anthus rubescens*
☐ Sprague's Pipit *Anthus spragueii*

BOMBYCILLIDAE

☐ Bohemian Waxwing *Bombycilla garrulus*
☐ Cedar Waxwing *Bombycilla cedrorum*

PTILOGONATIDAE

☐ Gray Silky-flycatcher *Ptilogonys cinereus*
☐ Phainopepla *Phainopepla nitens*

PEUCEDRAMIDAE

☐ Olive Warbler *Peucedramus taeniatus*

PARULIDAE

☐ Bachman's Warbler *Vermivora bachmanii*
☐ Blue-winged Warbler *Vermivora pinus*
☐ Golden-winged Warbler *Vermivora chrysoptera*
☐ Tennessee Warbler *Vermivora peregrina*
☐ Orange-crowned Warbler *Vermivora celata*
☐ Nashville Warbler *Vermivora ruficapilla*
☐ Virginia's Warbler *Vermivora virginiae*
☐ Colima Warbler *Vermivora crissalis*

☐ Lucy's Warbler *Vermivora luciae*
☐ Crescent-chested Warbler *Parula superciliosa*
☐ Northern Parula *Parula americana*
☐ Tropical Parula *Parula pitiayumi*
☐ Yellow Warbler *Dendroica petechia*
☐ Chestnut-sided Warbler *Dendroica pensylvanica*
☐ Magnolia Warbler *Dendroica magnolia*
☐ Cape May Warbler *Dendroica tigrina*
☐ Black-throated Blue Warbler *Dendroica caerulescens*
☐ Yellow-rumped Warbler *Dendroica coronata*
☐ Black-throated Gray Warbler *Dendroica nigrescens*
☐ Golden-cheeked Warbler *Dendroica chrysoparia*
☐ Black-throated Green Warbler *Dendroica virens*
☐ Townsend's Warbler *Dendroica townsendi*
☐ Hermit Warbler *Dendroica occidentalis*
☐ Blackburnian Warbler *Dendroica fusca*
☐ Yellow-throated Warbler *Dendroica dominica*
☐ Grace's Warbler *Dendroica graciae*
☐ Pine Warbler *Dendroica pinus*
☐ Kirtland's Warbler *Dendroica kirtlandii*
☐ Prairie Warbler *Dendroica discolor*
☐ Palm Warbler *Dendroica palmarum*
☐ Bay-breasted Warbler *Dendroica castanea*
☐ Blackpoll Warbler *Dendroica striata*
☐ Cerulean Warbler *Dendroica cerulea*
☐ Black-and-white Warbler *Mniotilta varia*
☐ American Redstart *Setophaga ruticilla*
☐ Prothonotary Warbler *Protonotaria citrea*
☐ Worm-eating Warbler *Helmitheros vermivorus*
☐ Swainson's Warbler *Limnothlypis swainsonii*
☐ Ovenbird *Seiurus aurocapillus*
☐ Northern Waterthrush *Seiurus noveboracensis*
☐ Louisiana Waterthrush *Seiurus motacill*
☐ Kentucky Warbler *Oporornis formosus*
☐ Connecticut Warbler *Oporornis agilis*
☐ Mourning Warbler *Oporornis philadelphia*

☐ MacGillivray's Warbler *Oporornis tolmiei*
☐ Common Yellowthroat *Geothlypis trichas*
☐ Gray-crowned Yellowthroat *Geothlypis poliocephala*
☐ Hooded Warbler *Wilsonia citrina*
☐ Wilson's Warbler *Wilsonia pusilla*
☐ Canada Warbler *Wilsonia canadensis*
☐ Red-faced Warbler *Cardellina rubrifrons*
☐ Painted Redstart *Myioborus pictus*
☐ Slate-throated Redstart *Myioborus miniatus*
☐ Fan-tailed Warbler *Euthlypis lachrymosa*
☐ Golden-crowned Warbler *Basileuterus culicivorus*
☐ Rufous-capped Warbler *Basileuterus rufifrons*
☐ Yellow-breasted Chat *Icteria virens*

COEREBIDAE

☐ Bananaquit *Coereba flaveola*

THRAUPIDAE

☐ Hepatic Tanager *Piranga flava*
☐ Summer Tanager *Piranga rubra*
☐ Scarlet Tanager *Piranga olivacea*
☐ Western Tanager *Piranga ludoviciana*
☐ Flame-colored Tanager *Piranga bidentata*
☐ Stripe-headed Tanager *Spindalis zena*

EMBERIZIDAE

☐ White-collared Seedeater *Sporophila torqueola*
☐ Yellow-faced Grassquit *Tiaris olivacea*
☐ Black-faced Grassquit *Tiaris bicolor*
☐ Olive Sparrow *Arremonops rufivirgatus*
☐ Green-tailed Towhee *Pipilo chlorurus*
☐ Spotted Towhee *Pipilo maculatus*
☐ Eastern Towhee *Pipilo erythrophthalmus*
☐ Canyon Towhee *Pipilo fuscus*
☐ California Towhee *Pipilo crissalis*
☐ Abert's Towhee *Pipilo aberti*
☐ Rufous-winged Sparrow *Aimophila carpalis*
☐ Cassin's Sparrow *Aimophila cassinii*
☐ Bachman's Sparrow *Aimophila aestivalis*
☐ Botteri's Sparrow *Aimophila botterii*

☐ Rufous-crowned Sparrow *Aimophila ruficeps*
☐ Five-striped Sparrow *Aimophila quinquestriata*
☐ American Tree Sparrow *Spizella arborea*
☐ Chipping Sparrow *Spizella passerina*
☐ Clay-colored Sparrow *Spizella pallida*
☐ Brewer's Sparrow *Spizella breweri*
☐ Field Sparrow *Spizella pusilla*
☐ Worthen's Sparrow *Spizella wortheni*
☐ Black-chinned Sparrow *Spizella atrogularis*
☐ Vesper Sparrow *Pooecetes gramineus*
☐ Lark Sparrow *Chondestes grammacus*
☐ Black-throated Sparrow *Amphispiza bilineata*
☐ Sage Sparrow *Amphispiza belli*
☐ Lark Bunting *Calamospiza melanocorys*
☐ Savannah Sparrow *Passerculus sandwichensis*
☐ Grasshopper Sparrow *Ammodramas savannarum*
☐ Baird's Sparrow *Ammodramus bairdii*
☐ Henslow's Sparrow *Ammodramus henslowii*
☐ Le Conte's Sparrow *Ammodramus leconteii*
☐ Nelson's Sharp-tailed Sparrow *Ammodramus nelsoni*
☐ Saltmarsh Sharp-tailed Sparrow *Ammodramus caudacutus*
☐ Seaside Sparrow *Ammodramus maritimus*
☐ Fox Sparrow *Passerella iliaca*
☐ Song Sparrow *Melospiza melodia*
☐ Lincoln's Sparrow *Melospiza lincolnii*
☐ Swamp Sparrow *Melospiza georgiana*
☐ White-throated Sparrow *Zonotrichia albicollis*
☐ Harris's Sparrow *Zonotrichia querula*
☐ White-crowned Sparrow *Zonotrichia leucophrys*
☐ Golden-crowned Sparrow *Zonotrichia atricapilla*
☐ Dark-eyed Junco *Junco hyemalis*
☐ Yellow-eyed Junco *Junco phaeonotus*
☐ McCown's Longspur *Calcarius mccownii*
☐ Lapland Longspur *Calcarius lapponicus*
☐ Smith's Longspur *Calcarius pictus*
☐ Chestnut-collared Longspur *Calcarius ornatus*
☐ Pine Bunting *Emberiza leucocephalos*

- ☐ Little Bunting *Emberiza pusilla*
- ☐ Rustic Bunting *Emberiza rustica*
- ☐ Yellow-breasted Bunting *Emberiza aureola*
- ☐ Gray Bunting *Emberiza variabilis*
- ☐ Pallas's Bunting *Emberiza pallasi*
- ☐ Reed Bunting *Emberiza schoeniclus*
- ☐ Snow Bunting *Plectrophenax nivalis*
- ☐ McKay's Bunting *Plectrophenax hyperboreus*

CARDINALIDAE

- ☐ Crimson-collared Grosbeak *Rhodothraupis celaeno*
- ☐ Northern Cardinal *Cardinalis cardinalis*
- ☐ Pyrrhuloxia *Cardinalis sinuatus*
- ☐ Yellow Grosbeak *Pheucticus chrysopeplus*
- ☐ Rose-breasted Grosbeak *Pheucticus ludovicianus*
- ☐ Black-headed Grosbeak *Pheucticus melanocephalus*
- ☐ Blue Bunting *Cyanocompsa parellina*
- ☐ Blue Grosbeak *Guiraca caerulea*
- ☐ Lazuli Bunting *Passerina amoena*
- ☐ Indigo Bunting *Passerina cyanea*
- ☐ Varied Bunting *Passerina versicolor*
- ☐ Painted Bunting *Passerina ciris*
- ☐ Dickcissel *Spiza americana*

ICTERIDAE

- ☐ Bobolink *Dolichonyx oryzivorus*
- ☐ Red-winged Blackbird *Agelaius phoeniceus*
- ☐ Tricolored Blackbird *Agelaius tricolor*
- ☐ Tawny-shouldered Blackbird *Agelaius humeralis*
- ☐ Eastern Meadowlark *Sturnella magna*
- ☐ Western Meadowlark *Sturnella neglecta*
- ☐ Yellow-headed Blackbird *Xanthocephalus xanthocephalus*
- ☐ Rusty Blackbird *Euphagus carolinus*
- ☐ Brewer's Blackbird *Euphagus cyanocephalus*
- ☐ Common Grackle *Quiscalus quiscula*
- ☐ Boat-tailed Grackle *Quiscalus major*
- ☐ Great-tailed Grackle *Quiscalus mexicanus*
- ☐ Shiny Cowbird *Molothrus bonariensis*
- ☐ Bronzed Cowbird *Molothrus aeneus*
- ☐ Brown-headed Cowbird *Molothrus ater*
- ☐ Black-vented Oriole *Icterus wagleri*

- ☐ Orchard Oriole *Icterus spurius*
- ☐ Hooded Oriole *Icterus cucullatus*
- ☐ Streak-backed Oriole *Icterus pustulatus*
- ☐ Spot-breasted Oriole *Icterus pectoralis*
- ☐ Altamira Oriole *Icterus gularis*
- ☐ Audubon's Oriole *Icterus graduacauda*
- ☐ Baltimore Oriole *Icterus galbula*
- ☐ Bullock's Oriole *Icterus bullockii*
- ☐ Scott's Oriole *Icterus parisorum*

FRINGILLIDAE

- ☐ Common Chaffinch *Fringilla coelebs*
- ☐ Brambling *Fringilla montifringilla*
- ☐ Gray-crowned Rosy-Finch *Leucosticte tephrocotis*
- ☐ Black Rosy-Finch *Leucosticte atrata*
- ☐ Brown-capped Rosy-Finch *Leucosticte australis*
- ☐ Pine Grosbeak *Pinicola enucleator*
- ☐ Common Rosefinch *Carpodacus erythrinus*
- ☐ Purple Finch *Carpodacus purpureus*
- ☐ Cassin's Finch *Carpodacus cassinii*
- ☐ House Finch *Carpodacus mexicanus*
- ☐ Red Crossbill *Loxia curvirostra*
- ☐ White-winged Crossbill *Loxia leucoptera*
- ☐ Common Redpoll *Carduelis flammea*
- ☐ Hoary Redpoll *Carduelis hornemanni*
- ☐ Eurasian Siskin *Carduelis spinus*
- ☐ Pine Siskin *Carduelis pinus*
- ☐ Lesser Goldfinch *Carduelis psaltria*
- ☐ Lawrence's Goldfinch *Carduelis lawrencei*
- ☐ American Goldfinch *Carduelis tristis*
- ☐ Oriental Greenfinch *Carduelis sinica*
- ☐ Eurasian Bullfinch *Pyrrhula pyrrhula*
- ☐ Evening Grosbeak *Coccothraustes vespertinus*
- ☐ Hawfinch *Coccothraustes coccothraustes*

PASSERIDAE

- ☐ House Sparrow *Passer domesticus*
- ☐ Eurasian Tree Sparrow *Passer montanus*

Loons (Family Gaviidae)

Red-throated Loon *Gavia stellata*

DATE   LOCATION

Pacific Loon *Gavia pacifica*

DATE   LOCATION

Arctic Loon *Gavia arctica*

DATE   LOCATION

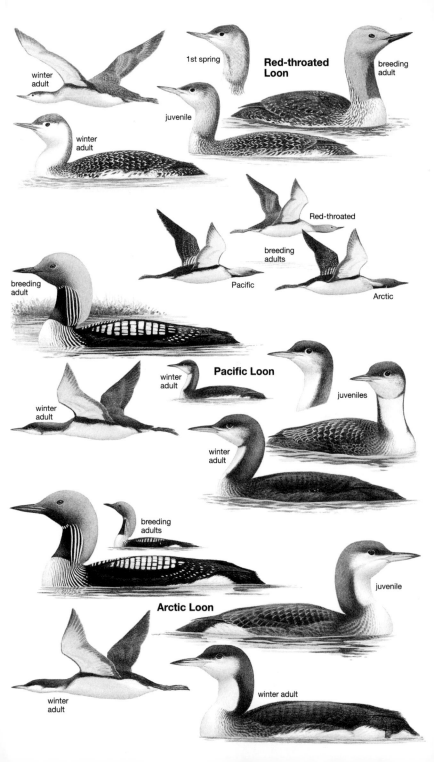

winter adult

1st spring

Red-throated Loon

breeding adult

juvenile

winter adult

Red-throated

breeding adults

Pacific

Arctic

breeding adult

winter adult

Pacific Loon

juveniles

winter adult

winter adult

breeding adults

Arctic Loon

juvenile

winter adult

winter adult

winter adult

Common Loon *Gavia immer*

DATE   LOCATION

Yellow-billed Loon *Gavia adamsii*

DATE   LOCATION

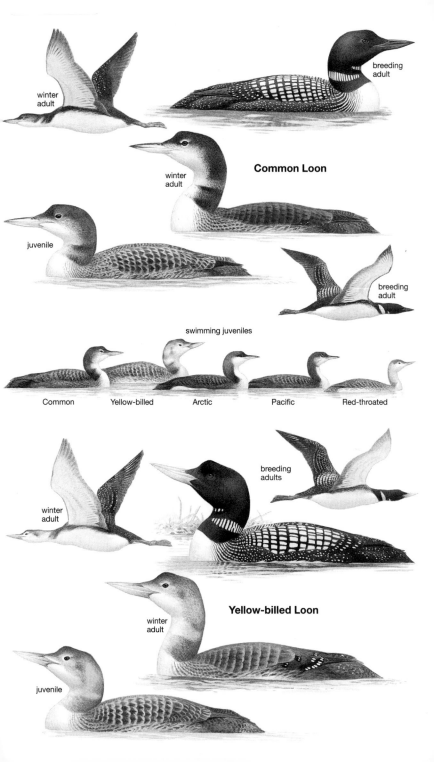

winter adult

breeding adult

Common Loon

winter adult

juvenile

breeding adult

swimming juveniles

Common   Yellow-billed   Arctic   Pacific   Red-throated

breeding adults

winter adult

Yellow-billed Loon

winter adult

juvenile

Grebes (Family Podicipedidae)

Horned Grebe *Podiceps auritus*

DATE   LOCATION

Eared Grebe *Podiceps nigricollis*

DATE   LOCATION

Pied-billed Grebe *Podilymbus podiceps*

DATE   LOCATION

Least Grebe *Tachybaptus dominicus*

DATE   LOCATION

Horned Grebe

breeding adult

winter

Eared Grebe

winter

breeding adult

Pied-billed Grebe

breeding

winter

Least Grebe

breeding

winter

Red-necked Grebe *Podiceps grisegena*

DATE   LOCATION

Clark's Grebe *Aechmophorus clarkii*

DATE   LOCATION

Western Grebe *Aechmophorus occidentalis*

DATE   LOCATION

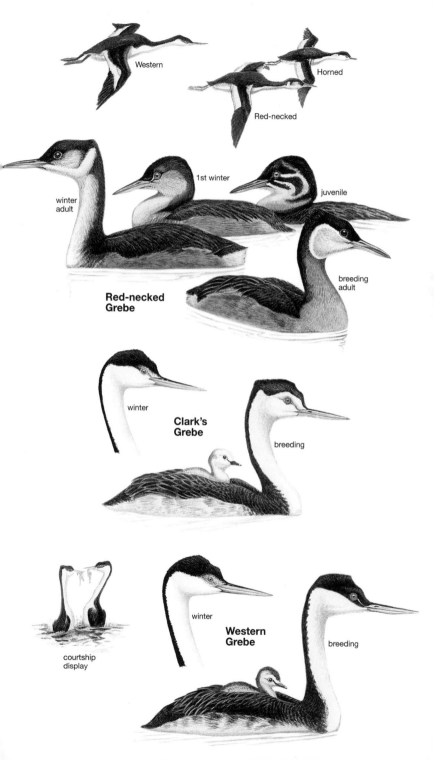

Western

Horned

Red-necked

winter
adult

1st winter

juvenile

**Red-necked
Grebe**

breeding
adult

winter

**Clark's
Grebe**

breeding

courtship
display

winter

**Western
Grebe**

breeding

Albatrosses (Family Diomedeidae)

Short-tailed Albatross *Phoebastria albatrus*

DATE
LOCATION

Shy Albatross *Thalassarche cauta*

DATE
LOCATION

Laysan Albatross *Phoebastria immutabilis*

DATE
LOCATION

Black-footed Albatross *Phoebastria nigripes*

DATE
LOCATION

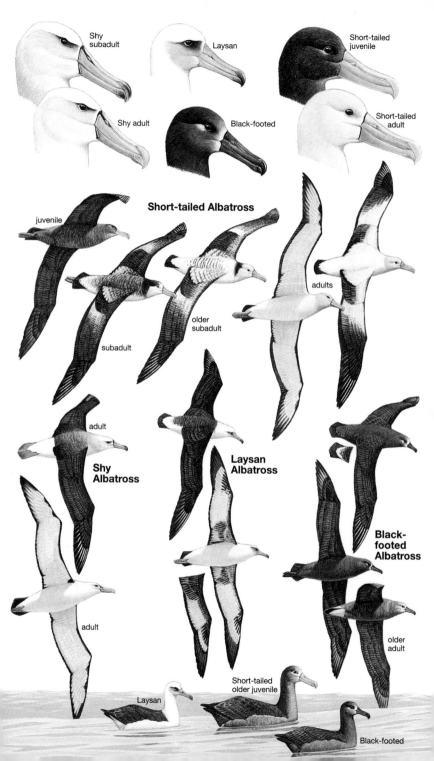

Shy subadult

Shy adult

Laysan

Black-footed

Short-tailed juvenile

Short-tailed adult

Short-tailed Albatross

juvenile

subadult

older subadult

adults

Shy Albatross

adult

adult

Laysan Albatross

Black-footed Albatross

older adult

Laysan

Short-tailed older juvenile

Black-footed

Yellow-nosed Albatross *Thalassarche chlororhynchos*

DATE   LOCATION

Black-browed Albatross *Thalassarche melanophris*

DATE   LOCATION

Shearwaters, Petrels (Family Procellariidae)

Northern Fulmar *Fulmarus glacialis*

DATE   LOCATION

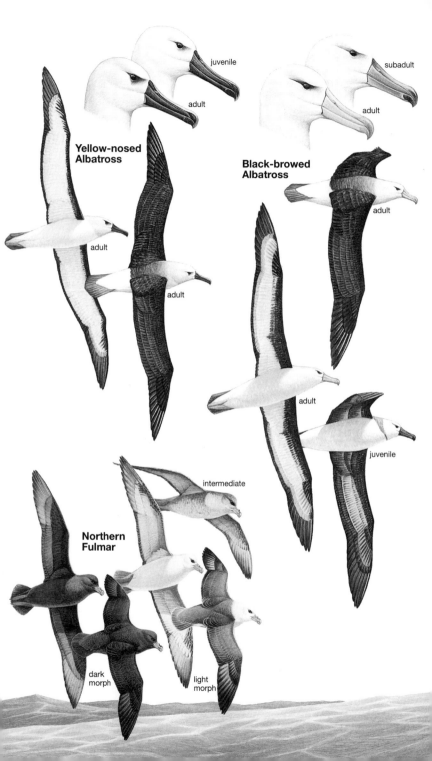

Yellow-nosed Albatross

juvenile

adult

adult

adult

Black-browed Albatross

subadult

adult

adult

adult

juvenile

Northern Fulmar

intermediate

dark morph

light morph

Gadfly Petrels

Black-capped Petrel *Pterodroma hasitata*

DATE   LOCATION

Fea's Petrel *Pterodroma feae*

DATE   LOCATION

Bermuda Petrel *Pterodroma cahow*

DATE   LOCATION

Herald Petrel *Pterodroma arminjoniana*

DATE   LOCATION

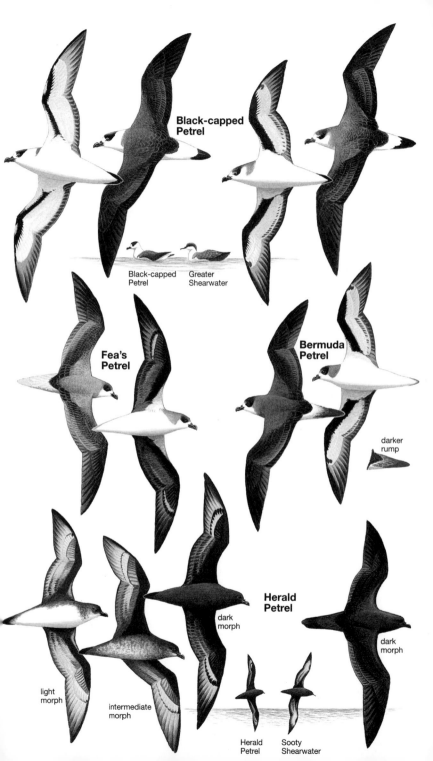

Black-capped Petrel

Black-capped Petrel   Greater Shearwater

Fea's Petrel

Bermuda Petrel

darker rump

Herald Petrel

dark morph

dark morph

light morph

intermediate morph

Herald Petrel   Sooty Shearwater

Dark-rumped Petrel *Pterodroma phaeopygia*

DATE   LOCATION

Murphy's Petrel *Pterodroma ultima*

DATE   LOCATION

Mottled Petrel *Pterodroma inexpectata*

DATE   LOCATION

Cook's Petrel *Pterodroma cookii*

DATE   LOCATION

Stejneger's Petrel *Pterodroma longirostris*

DATE   LOCATION

Dark-rumped
Petrel

Murphy's
Petrel

Mottled
Petrel

Cook's
Petrel

Stejneger's
Petrel

Streaked Shearwater *Calonectris leucomelas*

DATE   LOCATION

Buller's Shearwater *Puffinus bulleri*

DATE   LOCATION

Pink-footed Shearwater *Puffinus creatopus*

DATE   LOCATION

Black-vented Shearwater *Puffinus opisthomelas*

DATE   LOCATION

Streaked Shearwater

Buller's Shearwater

molting Pink-footed

Pink-footed Shearwater

Black-vented Shearwater

Wedge-tailed Shearwater *Puffinus pacificus*

DATE   LOCATION

Flesh-footed Shearwater *Puffinus carneipes*

DATE   LOCATION

Bulwer's Petrel *Bulweris bulwerii*

DATE   LOCATION

Short-tailed Shearwater *Puffinus tenuirostris*

DATE   LOCATION

Sooty Shearwater *Puffinus griseus*

DATE   LOCATION

dark
morph

dark
morph

**Flesh-footed
Shearwater**

**Wedge-tailed
Shearwater**

light
morph

**Bulwer's
Petrel**

**Short-tailed
Shearwater**

Sooty Shearwater

Short-tailed

Sooty

Cory's Shearwater *Calonectris diomedea*

DATE   LOCATION

....

....

....

....

Greater Shearwater *Puffinus gravis*

DATE   LOCATION

....

....

....

....

Manx Shearwater *Puffinus puffinus*

DATE   LOCATION

....

....

....

....

Little Shearwater *Puffinus assimilis*

DATE   LOCATION

....

....

....

....

Audubon's Shearwater *Puffinus lherminieri*

DATE   LOCATION

....

....

....

....

Cory's Shearwater *borealis*

Cory's

Greater

Black-capped Petrel

Greater Shearwater

Manx Shearwater

Little Shearwater *baroli*

Audubon's Shearwater

Storm-Petrels (Family Hydrobatidae)

Wilson's Storm-Petrel *Oceanites oceanicus*

DATE   LOCATION

Band-rumped Storm-Petrel *Oceanodroma castro*

DATE   LOCATION

Leach's Storm-Petrel *Oceanodroma leucorhoa*

DATE   LOCATION

White-faced Storm-Petrel *Pelagodroma marina*

DATE   LOCATION

Band-rumped Storm-Petrel

Wilson's Storm-Petrel

Leach's Storm-Petrel

White-faced Storm-Petrel

| Wilson's | Band-rumped | Leach's west coast | | | Wedge-rumped |
| | | northern | intermediate | southern | |

Black Storm-Petrel *Oceanodroma melania*

DATE   LOCATION

Ashy Storm-Petrel *Oceanodroma homochroa*

DATE   LOCATION

Least Storm-Petrel *Oceanodroma microsoma*

DATE   LOCATION

Fork-tailed Storm-Petrel *Oceanodroma furcata*

DATE   LOCATION

Wedge-rumped Storm-Petrel *Oceanodroma tethys*

DATE   LOCATION

Black
Storm-Petrel

Ashy
Storm-Petrel

Least Storm-Petrel

Fork-tailed
Storm-Petrel

Wedge-rumped
Storm-Petrel

Frigatebirds (Family Fregatidae)

Magnificent Frigatebird *Fregata magnificens*
....

DATE   LOCATION
....
....
....
....
....
....

Tropicbirds (Family Phaethontidae)

White-tailed Tropicbird *Phaethon lepturus*
....

DATE   LOCATION
....
....
....
....
....

Red-billed Tropicbird *Phaethon aethereus*
....

DATE   LOCATION
....
....
....
....

Red-tailed Tropicbird *Phaethon rubricauda*
....

DATE   LOCATION
....
....
....
....

Magnificent Frigatebird

juvenile

adult ♂

displaying adult ♂

adult ♀

White-tailed Tropicbird

juvenile

adult

Red-billed Tropicbird

juvenile

adult

Red-tailed Tropicbird

juvenile

adult

Boobies, Gannets (Family Sulidae)

Red-footed Booby *Sula sula*

DATE   LOCATION

Brown Booby *Sula leucogaster*

DATE   LOCATION

Blue-footed Booby *Sula nebouxii*

DATE   LOCATION

Masked Booby *Sula dactylatra*

DATE   LOCATION

juvenile

adult white morphs

adult brown morph

Red-footed Booby

adult white-tailed brown morph

subadult brown morph

juvenile

adult white morph with black tail

adult ♂ *brewsteri*

Brown Booby

adult ♀

adult ♂

subadult ♀

juvenile

juveniles

adult

Blue-footed Booby

adults

Northern Gannet immature

Masked Booby

adult

adult

adult

juvenile

subadult

juvenile

subadult

Northern Gannet *Morus bassanus*

DATE   LOCATION

Pelicans (Family Pelecanidae)

American White Pelican *Pelecanus erythrorhynchos*

DATE   LOCATION

Brown Pelican *Pelecanus occidentalis*

DATE   LOCATION

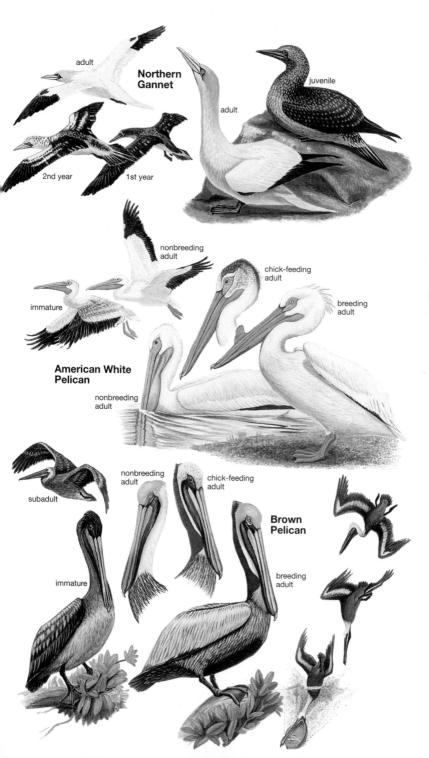

adult

Northern Gannet

adult

juvenile

2nd year   1st year

nonbreeding
adult

immature

chick-feeding
adult

breeding
adult

**American White
Pelican**

nonbreeding
adult

subadult

nonbreeding
adult

chick-feeding
adult

**Brown
Pelican**

immature

breeding
adult

Darters (Family Anhingidae)

Anhinga *Anhinga anhinga*

DATE   LOCATION

....

....

....

....

....

....

Cormorants (Family Phalacrocoracidae)

Neotropic Cormorant *Phalacrocorax brasilianus*

DATE   LOCATION

....

....

....

....

....

....

Great Cormorant *Phalacrocorax carbo*

DATE   LOCATION

....

....

....

....

....

....

breeding
adult ♂

♀

Anhinga

♀

Double-
crested
adult

Great adult

Neotropic
immature

breeding
adult

immature

nonbreeding
adult

eastern
Double-crested
breeding adult

Neotropic Cormorant

2nd year

Great Cormorant

breeding
adult

1st year

Double-crested Cormorant *Phalacrocorax auritus*

DATE .... LOCATION ....

....

....

....

....

....

....

Brandt's Cormorant *Phalacrocorax penicillatus*

DATE .... LOCATION ....

....

....

....

....

....

Pelagic Cormorant *Phalacrocorax pelagicus*

DATE .... LOCATION ....

....

....

....

....

....

Red-faced Cormorant *Phalacrocorax urile*

DATE .... LOCATION ....

....

....

....

....

....

1st year

western breeding adult

Double-crested Cormorant

Double-crested adult

Pelagic adult

Brandt's adult

Brandt's Cormorant

nonbreeding adult

nonbreeding adult

Pelagic Cormorant

1st year

breeding adult

1st year

breeding adult

breeding

1st year

Red-faced Cormorant

breeding adult

Herons, Bitterns (Family Ardeidae)

Least Bittern *Ixobrychus exilis*

DATE   LOCATION

American Bittern *Botaurus lentiginosus*

DATE   LOCATION

Black-crowned Night-Heron *Nycticorax nycticorax*

DATE   LOCATION

Yellow-crowned Night-Heron *Nyctanassa violacea*

DATE   LOCATION

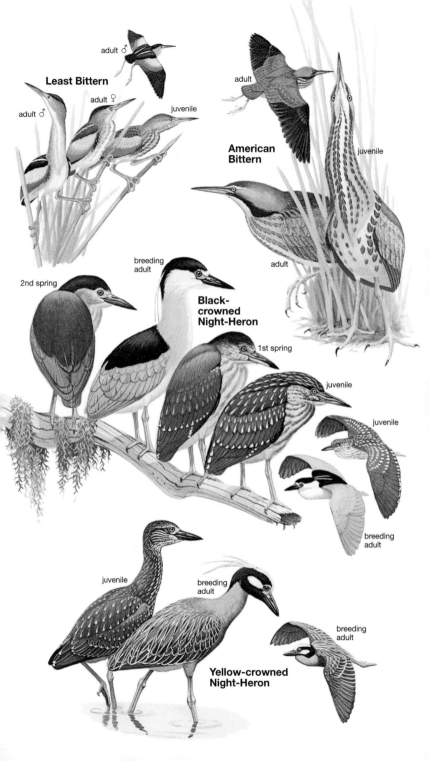

Least Bittern

adult ♂

adult ♂ adult ♀ juvenile

American Bittern

adult

juvenile

adult

2nd spring

breeding adult

Black-crowned Night-Heron

1st spring

juvenile

juvenile

breeding adult

juvenile

breeding adult

Yellow-crowned Night-Heron

breeding adult

Green Heron *Butorides virescens*

DATE   LOCATION

Tricolored Heron *Egretta tricolor*

DATE   LOCATION

Little Blue Heron *Egretta caerulea*

DATE   LOCATION

Reddish Egret *Egretta rufescens*

DATE   LOCATION

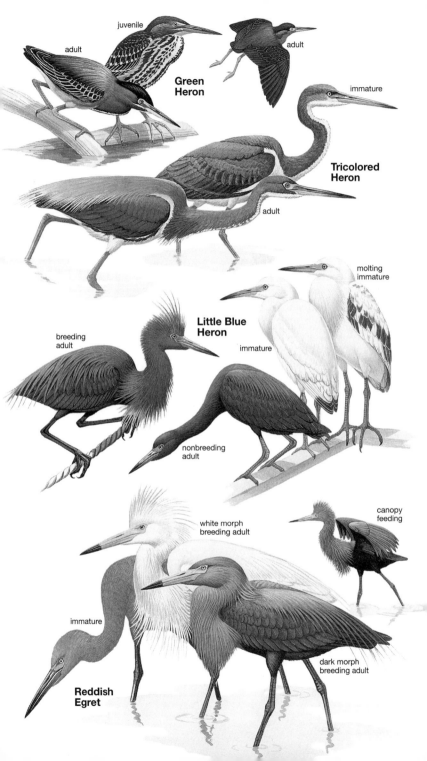

juvenile

adult

adult

Green Heron

immature

Tricolored Heron

adult

breeding adult

Little Blue Heron

molting immature

immature

nonbreeding adult

canopy feeding

white morph breeding adult

immature

dark morph breeding adult

Reddish Egret

Cattle Egret *Bubulcus ibis*

DATE   LOCATION

Little Egret *Egretta garzetta*

DATE   LOCATION

Snowy Egret *Egretta thula*

DATE   LOCATION

Great Egret *Ardea alba*

DATE   LOCATION

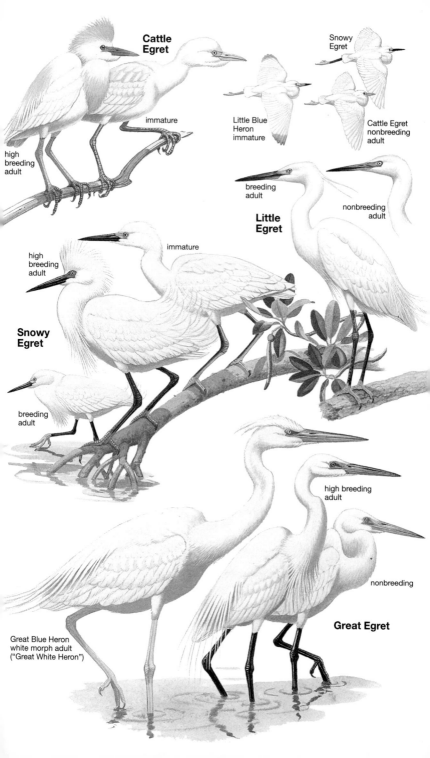

Cattle Egret

immature

high breeding adult

Snowy Egret

Little Blue Heron immature

Cattle Egret nonbreeding adult

breeding adult

nonbreeding adult

Little Egret

high breeding adult

immature

Snowy Egret

breeding adult

high breeding adult

nonbreeding

Great Blue Heron white morph adult ("Great White Heron")

Great Egret

Great Blue Heron *Ardea herodias*

DATE   LOCATION

Storks (Family Ciconiidae)

Wood Stork *Mycteria americana*

DATE   LOCATION

Jabiru *Jabiru mycteria*

DATE   LOCATION

Flamingos (Family Phoenicopteridae)

Greater Flamingo *Phoenicopterus ruber*

DATE   LOCATION

Great Blue Heron

breeding adult

adult

adult

"Wurdemann's Heron" adult

juvenile

juvenile

adult

Wood Stork

juvenile

Greater Flamingo

Jabiru

adult

immature

breeding adult

Ibises, Spoonbills (Family Threskiornithidae)

Glossy Ibis *Plegadis falcinellus*

DATE   LOCATION

White-faced Ibis *Plegadis chihi*

DATE   LOCATION

White Ibis *Eudocimus albus*

DATE   LOCATION

Roseate Spoonbill *Ajaia ajaja*

DATE   LOCATION

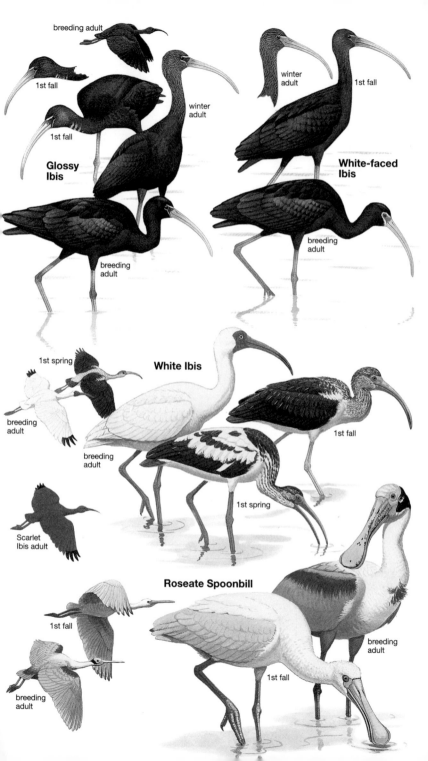

breeding adult

1st fall

1st fall

winter adult

Glossy Ibis

breeding adult

winter adult

1st fall

White-faced Ibis

breeding adult

1st spring

White Ibis

breeding adult

breeding adult

1st fall

Scarlet Ibis adult

1st spring

Roseate Spoonbill

1st fall

breeding adult

breeding adult

1st fall

Ducks, Geese, Swans (Family Anatidae)

Tundra Swan *Cygnus columbianus*

DATE   LOCATION

....

....

....

....

....

Trumpeter Swan *Cygnus buccinator*

DATE   LOCATION

....

....

....

....

....

Whooper Swan *Cygnus cygnus*

DATE   LOCATION

....

....

....

....

....

Mute Swan *Cygnus olor*

DATE   LOCATION

....

....

....

....

....

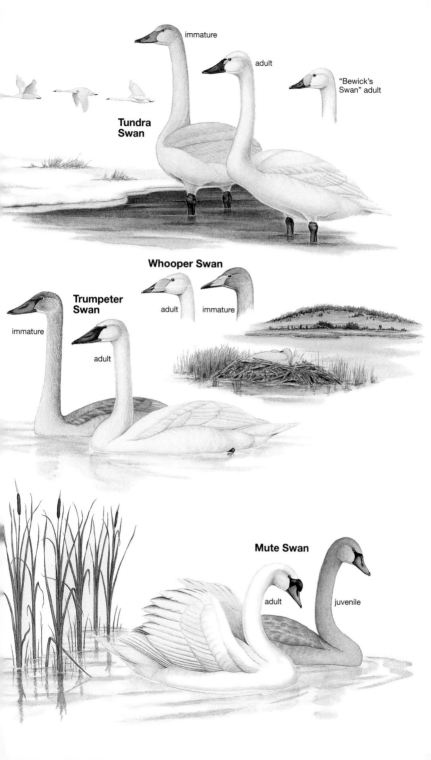

Tundra Swan

immature

adult

"Bewick's Swan" adult

Whooper Swan

Trumpeter Swan

immature

adult

adult

immature

Mute Swan

adult

juvenile

Greater White-fronted Goose *Anser albifrons*

DATE   LOCATION

Bean Goose *Anser fabalis*

DATE   LOCATION

Pink-footed Goose *Anser brachyrhynchus*

DATE   LOCATION

Greater White-fronted Goose

immature

tundra adult

taiga adult *elgasi*

Greenland adult *flavirostris*

adult *middendorffii*

Bean Goose

adult *serrirostris*

Pink-footed Goose

adult

Snow Goose *Chen caerulescens*

DATE   LOCATION

Ross's Goose *Chen rossii*

DATE   LOCATION

Emperor Goose *Chen canagica*

DATE   LOCATION

Snow Goose

blue morph adults

white morph immature

white morph adult

blue morph immature

Ross's Goose

white morph immature

white morph adult

blue morph adult

Emperor Goose

juvenile

adult

Canada Goose *Branta canadensis*

DATE   LOCATION

Brant *Branta bernicla*

DATE   LOCATION

Barnacle Goose *Branta leucopsis*

DATE   LOCATION

Canada Goose

canadensis

occidentalis

leucopareia

minima

hutchinsii

adult *hrota*

adult *nigricans*

Brant

hrota immature

Barnacle Goose

Whistling-Ducks

Fulvous Whistling-Duck *Dendrocygna bicolor*

DATE   LOCATION

Black-bellied Whistling-Duck *Dendrocygna autumnalis*

DATE   LOCATION

Perching Ducks

Wood Duck *Aix sponsa*

DATE   LOCATION

Muscovy Duck *Cairina moschata*

DATE   LOCATION

Fulvous Whistling-Duck

adult

Black-bellied Whistling-Duck

juvenile

Wood Duck

♀

juvenile ♂

♂

Muscovy Duck

juvenile ♀

adult ♂

adult ♂

domestic variety ♂

Dabbling Ducks

Mallard *Anas platyrhynchos*

DATE   LOCATION

Mottled Duck *Anas fulvigula*

DATE   LOCATION

American Black Duck *Anas rubripes*

DATE   LOCATION

Spot-billed Duck *Anas poecilorhyncha*

DATE   LOCATION

eclipse ♂

Mallard

juvenile

♀

♂

Mottled Duck

♂

"Mexican"-Mallard
intergrade

♂

American Black x
Mallard hybrid

♀

♂

**American
Black Duck**

**Spot-billed
Duck**

Gadwall *Anas strepera*

DATE   LOCATION

Falcated Duck *Anas falcata*

DATE   LOCATION

Green-winged Teal *Anas crecca*

DATE   LOCATION

Baikal Teal *Anas formosa*

DATE   LOCATION

Gadwall

♀

♂

♀

Falcated Duck

♂

crecca ♂

carolinensis ♀

carolinensis ♂

Green-winged Teal

Baikal Teal

bridled ♀

♂

♀

American Wigeon *Anas americana*

DATE   LOCATION

Eurasian Wigeon *Anas penelope*

DATE   LOCATION

Northern Pintail *Anas acuta*

DATE   LOCATION

White-cheeked Pintail *Anas bahamensis*

DATE   LOCATION

American Wigeon

eclipse ♂

♀

rufous morph ♀

ay morph ♀

Eurasian Wigeon

♂

immature ♂

♂

♀

Northern Pintail

♂

White-cheeked Pintail

Northern Shoveler *Anas clypeata*

DATE   LOCATION

Blue-winged Teal *Anas discors*

DATE   LOCATION

Garganey *Anas querquedula*

DATE   LOCATION

Cinnamon Teal *Anas cyanoptera*

DATE   LOCATION

Northern Shoveler

fall ♂

♂

♀

Blue-winged Teal

♀

♂

Garganey

♀

fall ♂

♂

Cinnamon Teal

♂

♀

Pochards

Canvasback *Aythya valisineria*

DATE   LOCATION

Common Pochard *Aythya ferina*

DATE   LOCATION

Redhead *Aythya americana*

DATE   LOCATION

Canvasback

♀

♂

Common Pochard

♀

♂

Redhead

♀

♂

Ring-necked Duck *Aythya collaris*

DATE   LOCATION

Tufted Duck *Aythya fuligula*

DATE   LOCATION

Greater Scaup *Aythya marila*

DATE   LOCATION

Lesser Scaup *Aythya affinis*

DATE   LOCATION

Ring-necked Duck

♂ ♀

Tufted Duck

♀

1st winter ♂

♂

Greater Scaup

1st winter ♂

♀

♂ ♀

Lesser Scaup

♂ ♀

Eiders

Common Eider *Somateria mollissima*

DATE   LOCATION

King Eider *Somateria spectabilis*

DATE   LOCATION

Spectacled Eider *Somateria fischeri*

DATE   LOCATION

Steller's Eider *Polysticta stelleri*

DATE   LOCATION

Common Eider

eclipse adult
♂ v-nigra

eclipse ♀
v-nigra

♀ dresseri

adult ♂
dresseri

1st winter ♂
dresseri

adult ♂ v-nigra

1st winter ♂

adult ♂

King Eider

♀

adult ♂

**Spectacled
Eider**

Common Eiders in flight

♀

Steller's Eider

1st winter ♂

adult ♂

♀

Sea Ducks

Black Scoter *Melanitta nigra*

DATE   LOCATION

White-winged Scoter *Melanitta fusca*

DATE   LOCATION

Surf Scoter *Melanitta perspicillata*

DATE   LOCATION

Harlequin Duck *Histrionicus histrionicus*

DATE   LOCATION

Black Scoter

1st winter ♂

adult ♂

adult ♀

White-winged Scoter

1st winter ♀

1st winter ♂

adult ♂

adult ♀

Surf Scoter

1st winter ♀

adult ♂

adult ♀

1st winter ♂

Harlequin Duck

♀

1st winter ♂

adult ♂

Oldsquaw *Clangula hyemalis*

DATE..LOCATION..

....

....

....

....

....

Barrow's Goldeneye *Bucephala islandica*

DATE..LOCATION..

....

....

....

....

Common Goldeneye *Bucephala clangula*

DATE..LOCATION..

....

....

....

....

Bufflehead *Bucephala albeola*

DATE..LOCATION..

....

....

....

....

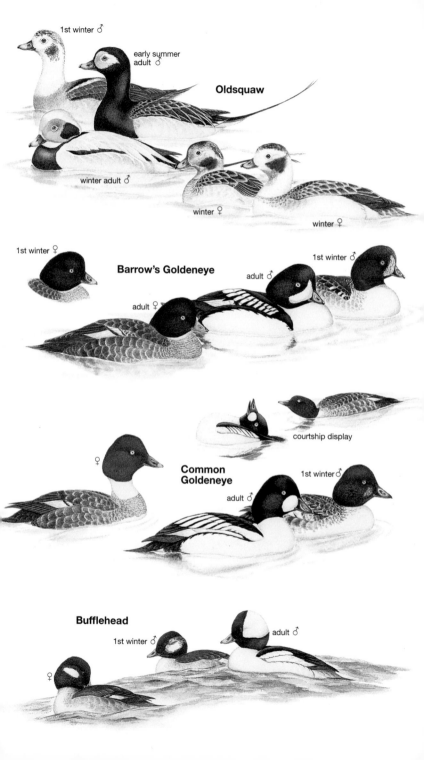

Oldsquaw

1st winter ♂

early summer adult ♂

winter adult ♂

winter ♀

winter ♀

Barrow's Goldeneye

1st winter ♀

adult ♀

adult ♂

1st winter ♂

Common Goldeneye

courtship display

♀

adult ♂

1st winter ♂

Bufflehead

♀

1st winter ♂

adult ♂

Mergansers

Common Merganser *Mergus merganser*

DATE   LOCATION

Red-breasted Merganser *Mergus serrator*

DATE   LOCATION

Hooded Merganser *Lophodytes cucullatus*

DATE   LOCATION

Smew *Mergellus albellus*

DATE   LOCATION

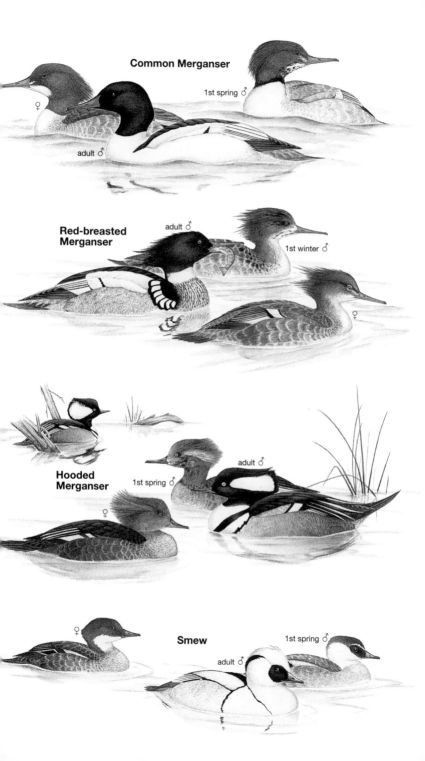

Common Merganser

♀

1st spring ♂

adult ♂

Red-breasted Merganser

adult ♂

1st winter ♂

♀

Hooded Merganser

1st spring ♂

adult ♂

♀

♀

Smew

adult ♂

1st spring ♂

Stiff-tailed Ducks

Ruddy Duck *Oxyura jamaicensis*

DATE   LOCATION

Masked Duck *Nomonyx dominicus*

DATE   LOCATION

Exotic Waterfowl

Ruddy Shelduck *Tadorna ferruginea*

DATE   LOCATION

Northern Shelduck *Tadorna tadorna*

DATE   LOCATION

Egyptian Goose *Alopochen aegyptiacus*

DATE   LOCATION

Chinese Goose *Anser cygnoides*

DATE   LOCATION

Mandarin Duck *Aix galericulata*

DATE   LOCATION

Domestic Goose *Anser "domesticus"*

DATE   LOCATION

Greylag Goose *Anser anser*

DATE   LOCATION

Bar-headed Goose *Anser indicus*

DATE   LOCATION

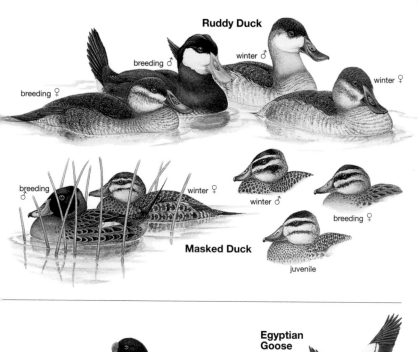

Ruddy Duck

breeding ♂

winter ♂

breeding ♀

winter ♀

breeding ♂

winter ♀

Masked Duck

winter ♂

breeding ♀

juvenile

Ruddy Shelduck

Northern Shelduck
♂

Egyptian Goose

Chinese Goose

Mandarin Duck
♀ ♂

Domestic Goose

Greylag Goose

Bar-headed Goose

Ducks in Flight

Northern Pintail
♂
♀

American Black Duck
♂

Eurasian Wigeon
adult ♂
gray mo ♀

American Wigeon
adult ♂
♀

Baikal Teal
♂
♀

Wood Duck
♂
♀

Ruddy Duck
breeding ♂
♀

Green-winged Teal
carolinensis ♂
carolinensis ♀

Mallard

♂

♀

Gadwall

♂

♀

Northern
Shoveler

♂

♂

♀

Falcated
Duck

♂

♀

Cinnamon
Teal

♂

Blue-winged
Teal

♂

♀

Garganey

♂

immature ♂

♀

Masked
Duck

breeding
♂

♀

Ducks in Flight

Common Merganser — adult ♂, ♀

Common Eider — dresseri ♂, dresseri ♀

Red-breasted Merganser — adult ♂, ♀

White-winged Scoter — adult ♂, adult ♀

Surf Scoter — adult ♂, immature ♀

Canvasback — ♂, ♀

Common Pochard — ♂, ♀

Redhead — ♂, ♀

Greater Scaup — ♂, ♀

Lesser Scaup — ♂, ♀

Tufted Duck — ♂, ♀

Ring-necked Duck — ♂, ♀

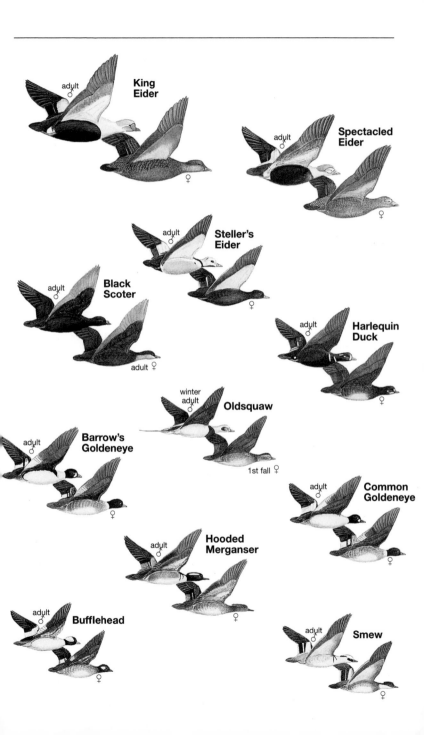

New World Vultures (Family Cathartidae)

Turkey Vulture *Cathartes aura*

DATE   LOCATION

Black Vulture *Coragyps atratus*

DATE   LOCATION

California Condor *Gymnogyps californianus*

DATE   LOCATION

Hawks, Kites, Eagles (Family Accipitridae)

Osprey *Pandion haliaetus*

DATE   LOCATION

Turkey Vulture
adults
adult
juvenile

adult

Black Vulture

juvenile

adult

California Condor
adult

adult

Osprey
adult
juvenile
adult

Mississippi Kite *Ictinia mississippiensis*

DATE   LOCATION

Swallow-tailed Kite *Elanoides forficatus*

DATE   LOCATION

White-tailed Kite *Elanus leucurus*

DATE   LOCATION

Mississippi Kite

juvenile

adult ♂

adult ♀

adult ♂

Swallow-tailed Kite

adults

juvenile

adult

White-tailed Kite

Snail Kite *Rostrhamus sociabilis*

DATE   LOCATION

Hook-billed Kite *Chondrohierax uncinatus*

DATE   LOCATION

Northern Harrier *Circus cyaneus*

DATE   LOCATION

Snail Kite

adult ♂

adult ♀

adult ♂

juvenile

black morph adult

black morph immature

adult ♂

molting immature

adult ♀

Hook-billed Kite

juvenile

juvenile

adult ♀

Northern Harrier

adult ♂

Golden Eagle *Aquila chrysaetos*

DATE   LOCATION

White-tailed Eagle *Haliaeetus albicilla*

DATE   LOCATION

Steller's Sea-Eagle *Haliaeetus pelagicus*

DATE   LOCATION

Bald Eagle *Haliaeetus leucocephalus*

DATE   LOCATION

Golden Eagle

juvenile

adult

adult

White-tailed Eagle

juvenile

adult

Steller's Sea-Eagle

adult

juvenile

Bald Eagle

juvenile

2nd year

3rd year

juvenile

adults

Accipiters

Sharp-shinned Hawk *Accipiter striatus*

DATE   LOCATION

Cooper's Hawk *Accipiter cooperii*

DATE   LOCATION

Northern Goshawk *Accipiter gentilis*

DATE   LOCATION

Sharp-shinned Hawk

adult ♂

juvenile ♀

juvenile

Cooper's Hawk

juvenile ♀

adult ♂

juvenile

Northern Goshawk

juvenile ♀

juvenile

adult ♂

Buteos

Common Black-Hawk *Buteogallus anthracinus*

DATE   LOCATION

Harris's Hawk *Parabuteo unicinctus*

DATE   LOCATION

Zone-tailed Hawk *Buteo albonotatus*

DATE   LOCATION

Short-tailed Hawk *Buteo brachyurus*

DATE   LOCATION

**Common
Black-Hawk**

adult

juvenile

juvenile

adult

Turkey Vulture
for comparison

juvenile

adult

**Harris's
Hawk**

adult

adult

juvenile

**Zone-tailed
Hawk**

adult

**Short-tailed
Hawk**

light morph
adult

light
morph
adult

dark
morph
adult

Broad-winged Hawk *Buteo platypterus*

DATE   LOCATION

Gray Hawk *Asturina nitida*

DATE   LOCATION

Red-shouldered Hawk *Buteo lineatus*

DATE   LOCATION

juveniles

juveniles

juveniles

dark morph adult

Broad-winged Hawk

juvenile

adult

juveniles

adult

Gray Hawk

juvenile

adult

adult *lineatus*

juvenile *lineatus*

adult *elegans*

juvenile *elegans*

juvenile *lineatus*

Red-shouldered Hawk

juvenile *lineatus*

adult *extimus*

adult *lineatus*

juvenile *lineatus*

juvenile *elegans*

Red-tailed Hawk *Buteo jamaicensis*

DATE   LOCATION

Swainson's Hawk *Buteo swainsoni*

DATE   LOCATION

Red-tailed Hawk

eastern adult *borealis*

eastern juvenile *borealis*

adult *harlani*

adult *krideri*

rufous morph adult *calurus*

eastern adult *borealis*

light morph juvenile

Swainson's Hawk

dark morph adult

light morph adult

light morph adult

intermediate morph adult

Rough-legged Hawk *Buteo lagopus*

DATE   LOCATION

Ferruginous Hawk *Buteo regalis*

DATE   LOCATION

White-tailed Hawk *Buteo albicaudatus*

DATE   LOCATION

Rough-legged Hawk

adult ♂

adult ♀

dark morph adult ♂

juvenile

Ferruginous Hawk

juvenile

adult

dark morph adult

adults

White-tailed Hawk

adult

juvenile

juvenile

adult

dark juvenile

Caracaras, Falcons (Family Falconidae)

Eurasian Hobby *Falco subbuteo*

DATE   LOCATION

Aplomado Falcon *Falco femoralis*

DATE   LOCATION

Crested Caracara *Carabara plancus*

DATE   LOCATION

Eurasian Hobby

adult

juvenile

adult

juvenile

adult

juvenile

Aplomado Falcon

juvenile ♀

adult ♂

adult

Crested Caracara

juvenile

adults

American Kestrel *Falco sparverius*

DATE   LOCATION

Eurasian Kestrel *Falco tinnunculus*

DATE   LOCATION

Merlin *Falco columbarius*

DATE   LOCATION

adult ♀

American Kestrel

adult ♂

adult ♂

juvenile ♂

adult ♂

Eurasian Kestrel

adult ♂

juvenile

♀

adult ♂

Merlin
columbarius

♀

adult ♂

♀ *suckleyi*

adult ♂
suckleyi

adult ♀
richardsonii

adult ♂

adult ♂ *richardsonii*

Prairie Falcon *Falco mexicanus*

DATE   LOCATION

Peregrine Falcon *Falco peregrinus*

DATE   LOCATION

Gyrfalcon *Falco rusticolus*

DATE   LOCATION

Prairie Falcon

adult ♂

♀

adult *pealei*

juvenile *pealei*

adult *pealei*

Peregrine Falcon

adult *anatum*

juvenile *anatum*

juvenile *tundrius*

adult *tundrius*

Gyrfalcon

gray morph juvenile

gray morph juvenile

dark morph adult

white morph adult

Female Hawks in Flight

White-tailed Kite
adult

Mississippi Kite
1st summer

Hook-billed Kite
adult

Snail Kite
adult

American Kestrel

Peregrine Falcon
adult

Merlin
columbarius

Gyrfalcon
gray morph juvenile

Prairie Falcon
adult

Sharp-shinned Hawk
adult

Cooper's Hawk
adult

Northern Goshawk
adult

Northern Harrier
adult

Gray Hawk
adult

Broad-winged Hawk
adult

Broad-winged Hawk
dark morph adult

Red-shouldered Hawk
adult *lineatus*

Female Hawks in Flight

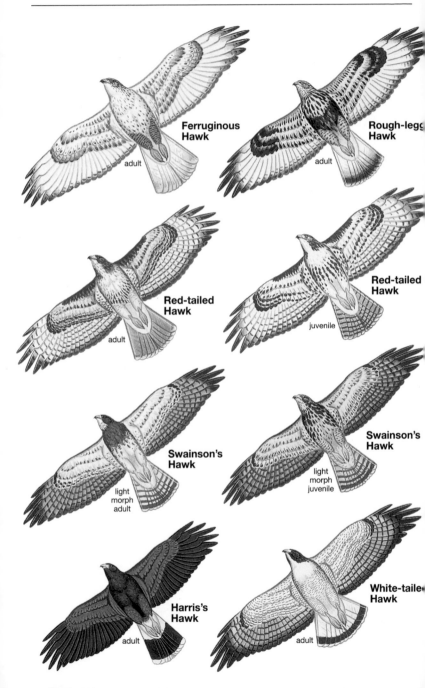

Ferruginous Hawk
adult

Rough-legged Hawk
adult

Red-tailed Hawk
adult

Red-tailed Hawk
juvenile

Swainson's Hawk
light morph adult

Swainson's Hawk
light morph juvenile

Harris's Hawk
adult

White-tailed Hawk
adult

Crested
Caracara
adult

Osprey
adult

Zone-tailed
Hawk
juvenile

Bald
Eagle
2nd
year

Common
Black-Hawk
adult

Golden
Eagle
adult

Black
Vulture
adult

Turkey
Vulture
adult

Chachalacas (Family Cracidae)

Plain Chachalaca *Ortalis vetula*

DATE   LOCATION

Partridges, Grouse, Turkeys (Family Phasianidae)

Chukar *Alectoris chukar*

DATE   LOCATION

Gray Partridge *Perdix perdix*

DATE   LOCATION

breeding ♂

Plain Chachalaca

Gray Partridge

♀

Chukar

♀

juvenile

♂

Ring-necked Pheasant *Phasianus colchicus*

DATE   LOCATION

Wild Turkey *Meleagris gallopavo*

DATE   LOCATION

Himalayan Snowcock *Tetraogallus himalayensis*

DATE   LOCATION

Ring-necked Pheasant

♂

♀

♀

Green Pheasant

♂

♀

♂

eastern *silvestris*

Wild Turkey

♀

♂

Himalayan Snowcock

♂

western *merriami*

Ruffed Grouse *Bonasa umbellus*

DATE   LOCATION

Spruce Grouse *Falcipennis canadensis*

DATE   LOCATION

Blue Grouse *Dendragapus obscurus*

DATE   LOCATION

gray morph ♂

red morph ♂

Ruffed Grouse

red morph ♀

red morph ♀

Spruce Grouse

gray morph ♀

"Franklin's Grouse" *franklinii*

♂

♂

coastal ♂ *fuliginosus*

northern Rockies ♂ *obscurus*

Blue Grouse

southern Rockies ♀ *richardsonii*

White-tailed Ptarmigan *Lagopus leucurus*

DATE   LOCATION

Rock Ptarmigan *Lagopus mutus*

DATE   LOCATION

Willow Ptarmigan *Lagopus lagopus*

DATE   LOCATION

White-tailed Ptarmigan

winter

summer ♀

molting fall ♂

summer ♂

Rock Ptarmigan

winter ♂

winter ♀

summer ♀

summer ♂

fall ♂

Willow Ptarmigan

summer ♀

molting spring ♂

winter

summer ♂

summer ♂

Greater Prairie-Chicken *Tympanuchus cupido*

DATE   LOCATION

Lesser Prairie-Chicken *Tympanuchus pallidicinctus*

DATE   LOCATION

Sharp-tailed Grouse *Tympanuchus phasianellus*

DATE   LOCATION

Sage Grouse *Centrocercus urophasianus*

DATE   LOCATION

Greater Prairie-Chicken

♀

displaying ♂

Lesser Prairie-Chicken

♀

displaying ♂

Sharp-tailed Grouse

♀

Sage Grouse

♂

♀

♀

displaying males on lek

New World Quail (Family Odontophoridae)

Gambel's Quail *Callipepla gambelii*

DATE   LOCATION

California Quail *Callipepla californica*

DATE   LOCATION

Mountain Quail *Oreortyx pictus*

DATE   LOCATION

Gambel's Quail

♂

♀

juvenile

Scaled x Gambel's hybrid

♂

♀ *californica*

coastal ♀ *brunescens*

California Quail

coastal juvenile *brunescens*

♂ *californica*

Mountain Quail

coastal ♂ *palmeri*

interior ♀

juvenile

Northern Bobwhite *Colinus virginianus*

DATE   LOCATION

Montezuma Quail *Cyrtonyx montezumae*

DATE   LOCATION

Scaled Quail *Callipepla squamata*

DATE   LOCATION

Northern Bobwhite

♂

♀

juvenile

"Masked Bobwhite"
♂ *ridgwayi*

Montezuma Quail

♂

♀

juvenile

Scaled Quail

juvenile

pallida ♂

South Texas ♂
castanogastris

Limpkin (Family Aramidae)

Limpkin *Aramus guarauna*

DATE   LOCATION

Rails, Gallinules, Coots (Family Rallidae)

King Rail *Rallus elegans*

DATE   LOCATION

Clapper Rail *Rallus longirostris*

DATE   LOCATION

Limpkin

King Rail

juvenile

crepitans

yumanensis

Clapper Rail

levipes

scottii

Virginia Rail *Rallus limicola*

DATE   LOCATION

Sora *Porzana carolina*

DATE   LOCATION

Yellow Rail *Coturnicops noveboracensis*

DATE   LOCATION

Black Rail *Laterallus jamaicensis*

DATE   LOCATION

Corn Crake *Crex crex*

DATE   LOCATION

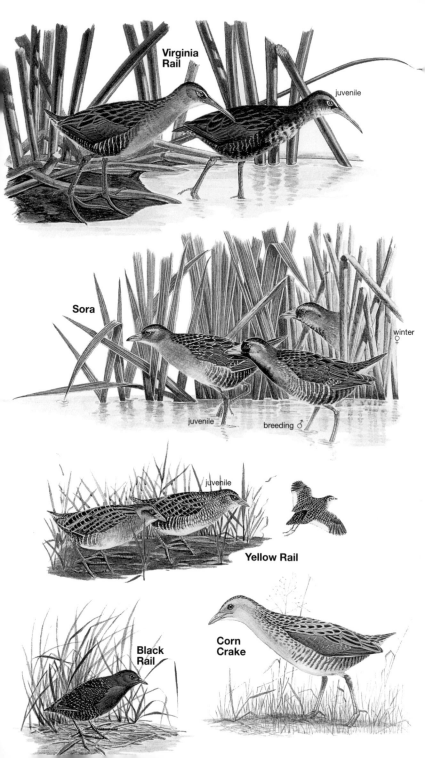

Virginia Rail

juvenile

Sora

winter ♀

juvenile

breeding ♂

juvenile

Yellow Rail

Black Rail

Corn Crake

Purple Gallinule *Porphyrula martinica*

DATE   LOCATION

Common Moorhen *Gallinula chloropus*

DATE   LOCATION

American Coot *Fulica americana*

DATE   LOCATION

Eurasian Coot *Fulica atra*

DATE   LOCATION

Purple Gallinule

juvenile

Common Moorhen

breeding

juvenile

winter

American Coot

immature

variant

Eurasian Coot

Cranes (Family Gruidae)

Sandhill Crane *Grus canadensis*

DATE   LOCATION

Common Crane *Grus grus*

DATE   LOCATION

Whooping Crane *Grus americana*

DATE   LOCATION

juvenile

adult

**Sandhill
Crane**

stained
adult

adult

juvenile

adult

**Common
Crane**

adult

adult

adult

juvenile

**Whooping
Crane**

Lapwings, Plovers (Family Charadriidae)

Black-bellied Plover *Pluvialis squatarola*

DATE   LOCATION

American Golden-Plover *Pluvialis dominica*

DATE   LOCATION

Pacific Golden-Plover *Pluvialis fulva*

DATE   LOCATION

European Golden-Plover *Pluvialis apricaria*

DATE   LOCATION

juveniles in flight

European   Pacific   American   Black-bellied

bright
juvenile   winter   breeding ♀

**Black-bellied
Plover**

juvenile   breeding ♂

bright
juvenile   juvenile   April ♂   breeding ♀

**American
Golden-Plover**

breeding ♂

juveniles   winter   breeding ♂

breeding
♀

**Pacific
Golden-Plover**

breeding ♂

juveniles   breeding ♂   breeding ♀

**European
Golden-Plover**

Snowy Plover *Charadrius alexandrinus*

DATE   LOCATION

Piping Plover *Charadrius melodus*

DATE   LOCATION

Wilson's Plover *Charadrius wilsonia*

DATE   LOCATION

Semipalmated Plover *Charadrius semipalmatus*

DATE   LOCATION

Common Ringed Plover *Charadrius hiaticula*

DATE   LOCATION

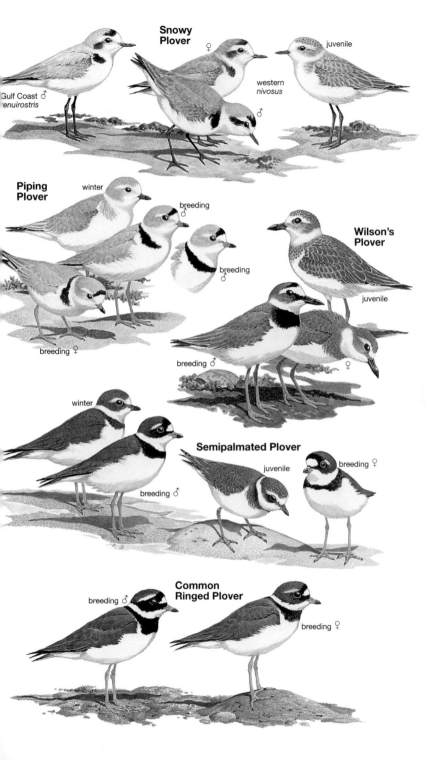

Snowy Plover

Gulf Coast ♂
enuirostris

♀

western
nivosus

♂

juvenile

Piping Plover

winter

breeding
♂

breeding
♂

breeding ♀

Wilson's Plover

juvenile

breeding ♂

♀

winter

breeding ♂

Semipalmated Plover

juvenile

breeding ♀

Common Ringed Plover

breeding ♂

breeding ♀

Mongolian Plover *Charadrius mongolus*

DATE   LOCATION

Little Ringed Plover *Charadrius dubius*

DATE   LOCATION

Killdeer *Charadrius vociferus*

DATE   LOCATION

Mountain Plover *Charadrius montanus*

DATE   LOCATION

Northern Lapwing *Vanellus vanellus*

DATE   LOCATION

Eurasian Dotterel *Charadrius morinellus*

DATE   LOCATION

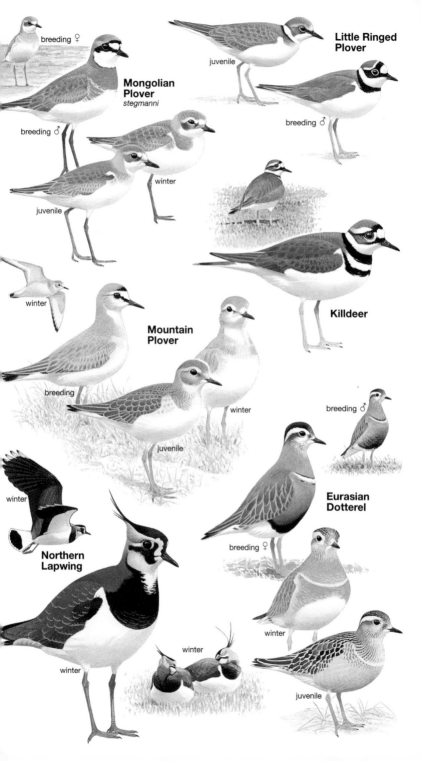

breeding ♀

Little Ringed Plover

juvenile

breeding ♂

breeding ♀

Mongolian Plover
stegmanni

breeding ♂

winter

juvenile

winter

Killdeer

Mountain Plover

winter

breeding

juvenile

breeding ♂

Eurasian Dotterel

winter

breeding ♀

Northern Lapwing

winter

winter

winter

juvenile

Jacanas (Family Jacanidae)

Northern Jacana *Jacana spinosa*

DATE   LOCATION

Oystercatchers (Family Haematopodidae)

Black Oystercatcher *Haematopus bachmani*

DATE   LOCATION

American Oystercatcher *Haematopus palliatus*

DATE   LOCATION

Stilts, Avocets (Family Recurvirostridae)

American Avocet *Recurvirostra americana*

DATE   LOCATION

Black-necked Stilt *Himantopus mexicanus*

DATE   LOCATION

Northern Jacana

adult

immature

adult

Black Oystercatcher

adult

adults

juvenile

American Oystercatcher

breeding ♀

juvenile ♂

breeding ♀

winter ♂

American Avocet

juvenile

Black-necked Stilt

♂

Sandpipers, Phalaropes (Family Scolopacidae)

Willet *Catoptrophorus semipalmatus*

DATE   LOCATION

Greater Yellowlegs *Tringa melanoleuca*

DATE   LOCATION

Lesser Yellowlegs *Tringa flavipes*

DATE   LOCATION

Common Redshank *Tringa totanus*

DATE   LOCATION

Common Greenshank *Tringa nebularia*

DATE   LOCATION

Spotted Redshank *Tringa erythropus*

DATE   LOCATION

Willet
western
inornatus

winter

breeding

juvenile

breeding

winter

juvenile

**Greater
Yellowlegs**

breeding

**Lesser
Yellowlegs**

winter

juvenile

juvenile

breeding

**Common
Redshank**

juvenile

**Common
Greenshank**

breeding

juvenile

breeding

winter

**Spotted
Redshank**

Wandering Tattler *Heteroscelus incanus*

DATE   LOCATION

Gray-tailed Tattler *Heteroscelus brevipes*

DATE   LOCATION

Green Sandpiper *Tringa ochropus*

DATE   LOCATION

Wood Sandpiper *Tringa glareola*

DATE   LOCATION

Wandering Tattler

breeding

winter

juvenile

Gray-tailed Tattler

breeding

juvenile

Solitary Sandpiper breeding

juvenile

breeding

Green Sandpiper

Green Sandpiper breeding

juvenile

breeding

Wood Sandpiper

breeding

Solitary Sandpiper *Tringa solitaria*

DATE   LOCATION

Spotted Sandpiper *Actitis macularia*

DATE   LOCATION

Common Sandpiper *Actitis hypoleucos*

DATE   LOCATION

Terek Sandpiper *Xenus cinereus*

DATE   LOCATION

Solitary Sandpiper

breeding

juvenile

1st winter

juvenile

Spotted Sandpiper

juvenile

breeding

breeding

juvenile

Common Sandpiper

juvenile

breeding

breeding

juvenile

Terek Sandpiper

Whimbrel *Numenius phaeopus*

DATE .... LOCATION ....

....

....

Eskimo Curlew *Numenius borealis*

DATE .... LOCATION ....

....

Little Curlew *Numenius minutus*

DATE .... LOCATION ....

....

Bristle-thighed Curlew *Numenius tahitiensis*

DATE .... LOCATION ....

....

Long-billed Curlew *Numenius americanus*

DATE .... LOCATION ....

....

Far Eastern Curlew *Numenius madagascariensis*

DATE .... LOCATION ....

....

Eurasian Curlew *Numenius arquata*

DATE .... LOCATION ....

....

....

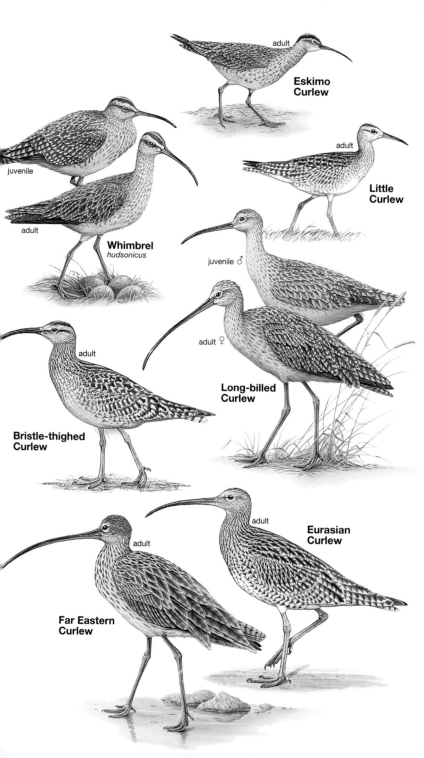

adult

Eskimo
Curlew

adult

Little
Curlew

juvenile

adult

Whimbrel
hudsonicus

juvenile ♂

adult ♀

Long-billed
Curlew

Bristle-thighed
Curlew

adult

adult

Eurasian
Curlew

adult

Far Eastern
Curlew

Marbled Godwit *Limosa fedoa*

DATE   LOCATION

Bar-tailed Godwit *Limosa lapponica*

DATE   LOCATION

Black-tailed Godwit *Limosa limosa*

DATE   LOCATION

Hudsonian Godwit *Limosa haemastica*

DATE   LOCATION

Marbled Godwit

winter

breeding

breeding ♂

Bar-tailed Godwit *baueri*

winter adult

juvenile

winter

Black-tailed Godwit *melanuroides*

breeding ♂

winter

breeding ♂

juvenile

Hudsonian Godwit

Ruddy Turnstone *Arenaria interpres*

DATE   LOCATION

Black Turnstone *Arenaria melanocephala*

DATE   LOCATION

Surfbird *Aphriza virgata*

DATE   LOCATION

Rock Sandpiper *Calidris ptilocnemis*

DATE   LOCATION

Purple Sandpiper *Calidris maritima*

DATE   LOCATION

Ruddy Turnstone

juvenile

winter

breeding ♂

breeding ♂

Black Turnstone

winter

breeding

winter

Surfbird

winter

juvenile

breeding

winter

Rock Sandpiper
tschuktschorum

winter

juvenile

breeding

breeding Pribilofs
ptilocnemis

Purple Sandpiper

juvenile

winter

breeding

Great Knot *Calidris tenuirostris*

DATE   LOCATION

Red Knot *Calidris canutus*

DATE   LOCATION

Sanderling *Calidris alba*

DATE   LOCATION

Dunlin *Calidris alpina*

DATE   LOCATION

Curlew Sandpiper *Calidris ferruginea*

DATE   LOCATION

Great Knot

juvenile

breeding

Red Knot

juvenile

winter

breeding

Sanderling

juvenile

winter

breeding

Dunlin

molting juvenile

winter

breeding

Curlew Sandpiper

juvenile

breeding ♂

Semipalmated Sandpiper *Calidris pusilla*

DATE   LOCATION

Western Sandpiper *Calidris mauri*

DATE   LOCATION

Least Sandpiper *Calidris minutilla*

DATE   LOCATION

White-rumped Sandpiper *Calidris fuscicollis*

DATE   LOCATION

Baird's Sandpiper *Calidris bairdii*

DATE   LOCATION

Semipalmated Sandpiper

breeding

juvenile

winter

Western Sandpiper

breeding

winter

juvenile

Least Sandpiper

winter

breeding

juvenile

White-rumped Sandpiper

fall molting adult

juvenile

breeding

Baird's Sandpiper

juvenile

breeding

Long-toed Stint *Calidris subminuta*

DATE   LOCATION

Little Stint *Calidris minuta*

DATE   LOCATION

Temminck's Stint *Calidris temminckii*

DATE   LOCATION

Red-necked Stint *Calidris ruficollis*

DATE   LOCATION

Spoonbill Sandpiper *Eurynorhynchus pygmeus*

DATE   LOCATION

Broad-billed Sandpiper *Limicola falcinellus*

DATE   LOCATION

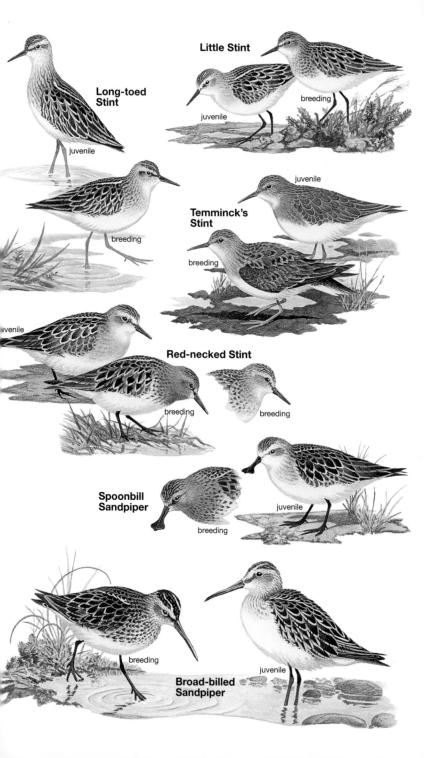

Long-toed Stint

juvenile

breeding

Little Stint

juvenile

breeding

Temminck's Stint

juvenile

breeding

Red-necked Stint

juvenile

breeding

breeding

Spoonbill Sandpiper

breeding

juvenile

Broad-billed Sandpiper

breeding

juvenile

Pectoral Sandpiper *Calidris melanotos*

DATE   LOCATION

Sharp-tailed Sandpiper *Calidris acuminata*

DATE   LOCATION

Upland Sandpiper *Bartramia longicauda*

DATE   LOCATION

Buff-breasted Sandpiper *Tryngites subruficollis*

DATE   LOCATION

Ruff *Philomachus pugnax*

DATE   LOCATION

breeding ♂

Pectoral Sandpiper

breeding ♀

juvenile

juvenile Sharp-tailed (center) with juvenile Pectorals

breeding adult

Sharp-tailed Sandpiper

juvenile

adult

Upland Sandpiper

juvenile

displaying adult

juvenile

Buff-breasted Sandpiper

breeding adult

summer molting ♂

breeding males

♀

Ruff

summer molting ♀

juvenile ♀

winter ♂

Dowitchers

Short-billed Dowitcher *Limnodromus griseus*

DATE   LOCATION

....

....

....

....

....

....

....

....

....

....

....

....

Long-billed Dowitcher *Limnodromus scolopaceus*

DATE   LOCATION

....

....

....

....

....

....

....

....

....

....

....

....

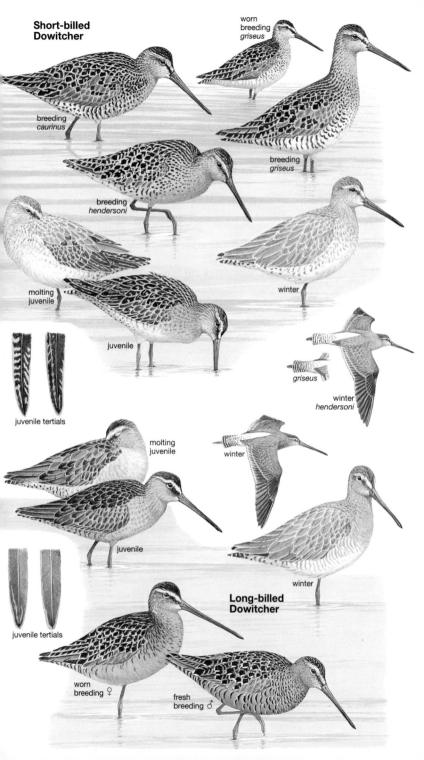

Short-billed Dowitcher

breeding *caurinus*

worn breeding *griseus*

breeding *griseus*

breeding *hendersoni*

molting juvenile

winter

juvenile

juvenile tertials

griseus

winter *hendersoni*

molting juvenile

winter

juvenile

juvenile tertials

winter

Long-billed Dowitcher

worn breeding ♀

fresh breeding ♂

Stilt Sandpiper *Calidris himantopus*

DATE   LOCATION

Common Snipe *Gallinago gallinago*

DATE   LOCATION

Pin-tailed Snipe *Gallinago stenura*

DATE   LOCATION

Jack Snipe *Lymnocryptes minimus*

DATE   LOCATION

American Woodcock *Scolopax minor*

DATE   LOCATION

Stilt Sandpiper breeding

juvenile

molting juvenile

winter

delicata underwing

displaying

delicata

gallinago underwing

Common Snipe

gallinago

Pin-tailed Snipe

underwing

American Woodcock

tail

Jack Snipe

Phalaropes

Wilson's Phalarope *Phalaropus tricolor*

DATE   LOCATION

Red-necked Phalarope *Phalaropus lobatus*

DATE   LOCATION

Red Phalarope *Phalaropus fulicaria*

DATE   LOCATION

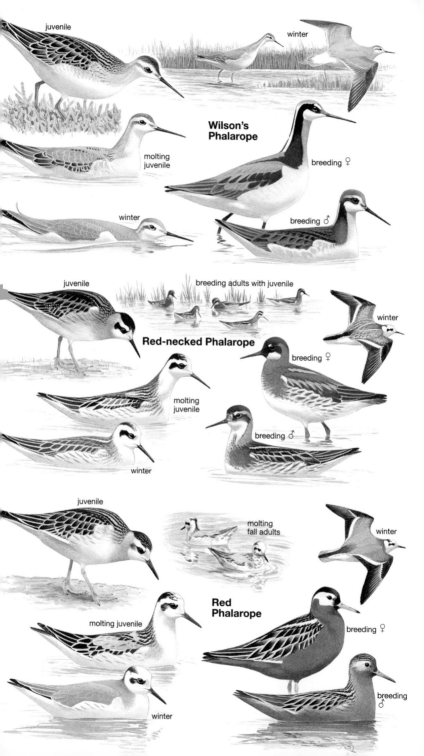

juvenile

winter

Wilson's Phalarope

molting juvenile

breeding ♀

breeding ♂

winter

juvenile

breeding adults with juvenile

Red-necked Phalarope

winter

breeding ♀

molting juvenile

breeding ♂

winter

juvenile

molting fall adults

winter

Red Phalarope

molting juvenile

breeding ♀

breeding ♂

winter

Shorebirds in Flight

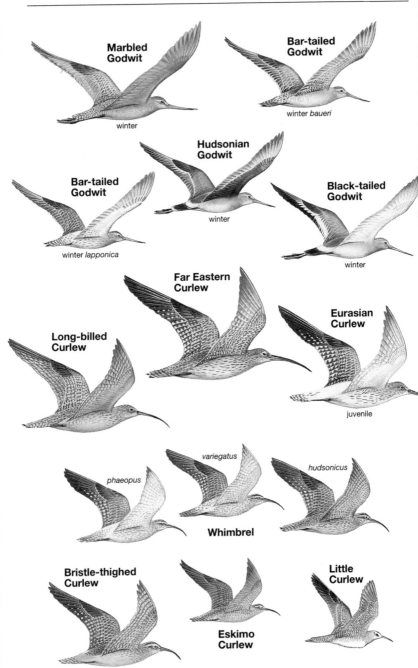

Marbled Godwit
winter

Bar-tailed Godwit
winter *baueri*

Hudsonian Godwit
winter

Bar-tailed Godwit
winter *lapponica*

Black-tailed Godwit
winter

Far Eastern Curlew

Eurasian Curlew
juvenile

Long-billed Curlew

phaeopus

variegatus

hudsonicus

Whimbrel

Bristle-thighed Curlew

Eskimo Curlew

Little Curlew

Willet winter

Greater Yellowlegs winter

Lesser Yellowlegs winter

een ndpiper juvenile

Wood Sandpiper juvenile

Solitary Sandpiper juvenile

Short-billed Dowitcher winter

Spotted Redshank winter

Common Greenshank winter

Common Redshank juvenile

Red Knot winter

Curlew Sandpiper juvenile

Stilt Sandpiper juvenile

Upland Sandpiper juvenile

Wilson's Phalarope juvenile

Buff-breasted Sandpiper juvenile

Shorebirds in Flight

Snowy Plover ♀

Piping Plover winter

Little Ringed Plover br

Semipalmated Plover juvenile

Common Ringed Plover juvenile

Mongolian Plover winter

Wilson's Plover ♀

Killdeer

Mountain Plover wi

Eurasian Dotterel juvenile

Pacific Golden-Plover juvenile

American Golden-Plover juvenile

European Golden-Plover juvenile

Black-bellied Plover juvenile

Rock Sandpiper winter

Purple Sandpiper winter

Dunlin winter

Sanderling winter

Red Phalarope winter

Red-necked Phalarope winter

Western Sandpiper winter

Semipalmated Sandpiper winter

Least Sandpiper winter

Temminck's Stint juvenile

Baird's Sandpiper juvenile

White-rumped Sandpiper juvenile

Pectoral Sandpiper juvenile

Sharp-tailed Sandpiper juvenile

Ruff juvenile ♀

Skuas, Gulls, Terns, Skimmers (Family Laridae)

Great Skua *Catharacta skua*

DATE   LOCATION

South Polar Skua *Catharacta maccormicki*

DATE   LOCATION

Great Skua

typical adult

dark adult

pale adult

juvenile

dark morph adult

intermediate morph adult

juvenile

South Polar Skua

juvenile

light morph adults

Jaegers

Pomarine Jaeger *Stercorarius pomarinus*

DATE   LOCATION

Parasitic Jaeger *Stercorarius parasiticus*

DATE   LOCATION

Long-tailed Jaeger *Stercorarius longicaudus*

DATE   LOCATION

Pomarine Jaeger

dark-morph breeding adult

light morph breeding adult

ght morph subadult

juvenile

Parasitic Jaeger

light morph breeding adult

dark morph breeding adult

light morph juveniles

light morph subadult

Long-tailed Jaeger

light morph juvenile

dark morph juvenile

breeding adult

subadult

Gulls

Heermann's Gull *Larus heermanni*

DATE   LOCATION

Franklin's Gull *Larus pipixcan*

DATE   LOCATION

Laughing Gull *Larus atricilla*

DATE   LOCATION

Heermann's Gull

breeding adult

winter adult

2nd winter

1st winter

breeding adult

breeding adult

winter adult

1st winter

Franklin's Gull

breeding adult

1st summer

breeding adult

2nd winter

Laughing Gull

breeding adult

winter adult

breeding adult

1st winter

juvenile

Bonaparte's Gull *Larus philadelphia*

DATE   LOCATION

Black-headed Gull *Larus ridibundus*

DATE   LOCATION

Little Gull *Larus minutus*

DATE   LOCATION

Ross's Gull *Rhodostethia rosea*

DATE   LOCATION

Bonaparte's Gull

breeding adult

winter adult

1st winter

winter adult

breeding adult

1st summer

winter adult

1st winter

winter adult

Black-headed Gull

breeding adult

1st winter

breeding adult

winter adult

Little Gull

Ross's Gull

winter adult

1st winter

breeding adult

Ring-billed Gull *Larus delawarensis*

DATE   LOCATION

Mew Gull *Larus canus*

DATE   LOCATION

Ring-billed Gull

winter adult

breeding adult

2nd winter

breeding adult

juvenile

1st winter

1st winter tail

1st winter tail

winter adult

2nd winter

breeding adults

juvenile

Mew Gull
brachyrhynchus

1st winter

kamtschatschensis

winter adult

1st winter

adult *kamtschatschensis*

winter adult

canus

1st winter

adult *canus*

California Gull *Larus californicus*

DATE   LOCATION

Black-tailed Gull *Larus crassirostris*

DATE   LOCATION

Band-tailed Gull *Larus belcheri*

DATE   LOCATION

Kelp Gull *Larus dominicanus*

DATE   LOCATION

California Gull

ding adult

winter adult

2nd winter

breeding adult

1st winter

pale juvenile

dark juvenile

Black-tailed Gull

breeding adult

winter adult

1st winter

2nd winter

breeding adult

Band-tailed Gull

breeding adult

winter adult

2nd winter

1st winter

breeding adult

Kelp Gull

moilting juvenile

2nd summer

winter adult

breeding adult

Herring Gull *Larus argentatus*

DATE   LOCATION

Yellow-legged Gull *Larus cachinnans*

DATE   LOCATION

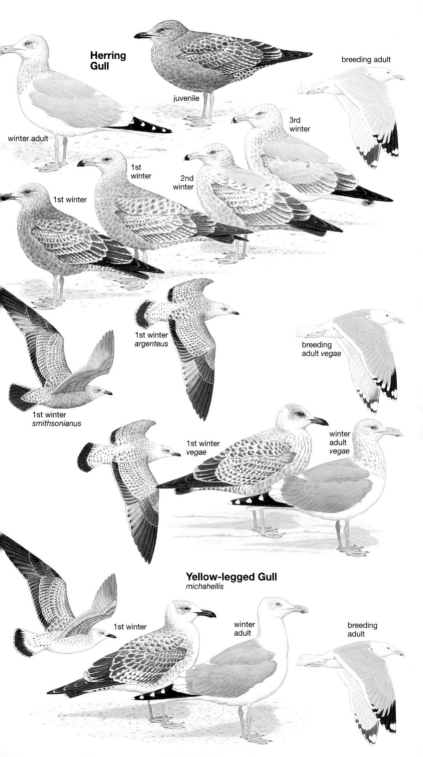

Herring Gull

juvenile

breeding adult

winter adult

3rd winter

1st winter

2nd winter

1st winter

1st winter *argenteus*

breeding adult *vegae*

1st winter *smithsonianus*

1st winter *vegae*

winter adult *vegae*

Yellow-legged Gull
michahellis

1st winter

winter adult

breeding adult

Glaucous Gull *Larus hyperboreus*

DATE   LOCATION

Iceland Gull *Larus glaucoides*

DATE   LOCATION

Thayer's Gull *Larus thayeri*

DATE   LOCATION

Glaucous Gull

breeding adult

2nd winter

winter adult

winter adult

1st winter

1st winter

Iceland Gull

1st winter

winter adult

breeding adult

winter adult

1st winter

2nd winter

2nd winter

winter adult

winter adult

breeding adult

Thayer's Gull

1st winter

1st winter

Yellow-footed Gull *Larus livens*

DATE   LOCATION

....

....

....

....

....

....

....

....

Western Gull *Larus occidentalis*

DATE   LOCATION

....

....

....

....

....

....

....

....

Glaucous-winged Gull *Larus glaucescens*

DATE   LOCATION

....

....

....

....

....

....

....

Yellow-footed Gull

2nd winter

adult

juvenile

adult

1st summer

Western Gull

southern 3rd winter *wymani*

southern winter adult *wymani*

southern breeding adult *wymani*

northern breeding adult *occidentalis*

juvenile

southern 2nd winter *wymani*

1st winter

Glaucous-winged x Western hybrid

1st winter

breeding adult

Glaucous-winged Gull

breeding adult

2nd winter

breeding adult

1st winter

Slaty-backed Gull *Larus schistisagus*

DATE · LOCATION

· ·

Lesser Black-backed Gull *Larus fuscus*

DATE · LOCATION

· ·

Great Black-backed Gull *Larus marinus*

DATE · LOCATION

· ·

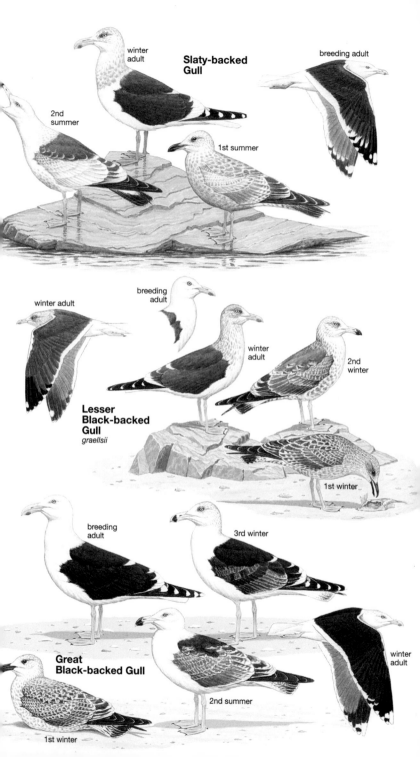

winter adult

Slaty-backed Gull

breeding adult

2nd summer

1st summer

winter adult

breeding adult

Lesser Black-backed Gull
graellsii

winter adult

2nd winter

1st winter

breeding adult

3rd winter

Great Black-backed Gull

winter adult

2nd summer

1st winter

Black-legged Kittiwake *Rissa tridactyla*

DATE   LOCATION

Red-legged Kittiwake *Rissa brevirostris*

DATE   LOCATION

Sabine's Gull *Xema sabini*

DATE   LOCATION

Ivory Gull *Pagophila eburnea*

DATE   LOCATION

Black-legged Kittiwake

winter adult

juvenile

breeding adult

Red-legged Kittiwake

breeding adult

breeding adult

juvenile

1st summer

breeding adult

molting adult

Sabine's Gull

juvenile

breeding adult

adult

Ivory Gull

1st winter

adult

Immature Gulls in Flight

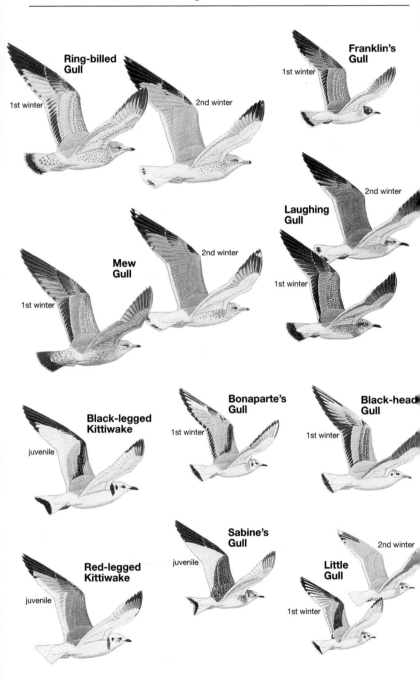

Ring-billed Gull

1st winter

2nd winter

Franklin's Gull

1st winter

2nd winter

Laughing Gull

1st winter

Mew Gull

1st winter

2nd winter

Black-legged Kittiwake

juvenile

Bonaparte's Gull

1st winter

Black-headed Gull

1st winter

Red-legged Kittiwake

juvenile

Sabine's Gull

juvenile

Little Gull

1st winter

2nd winter

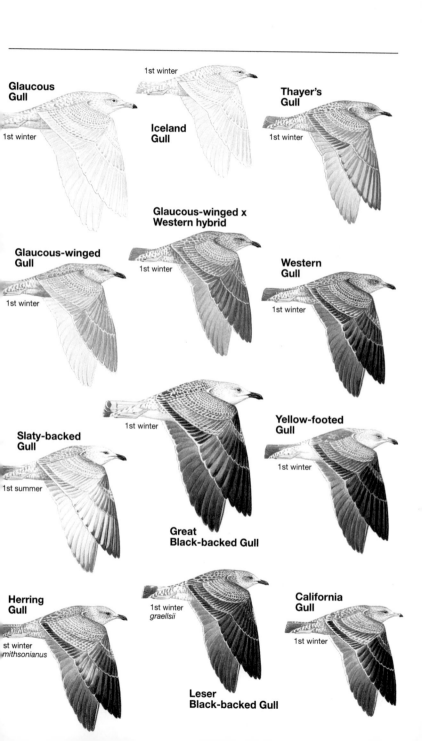

Glaucous Gull

1st winter

1st winter

Iceland Gull

Thayer's Gull

1st winter

Glaucous-winged x Western hybrid

1st winter

Glaucous-winged Gull

1st winter

Western Gull

1st winter

Slaty-backed Gull

1st winter

1st summer

Yellow-footed Gull

1st winter

Great Black-backed Gull

Herring Gull

st winter
mithsonianus

1st winter
graellsii

California Gull

1st winter

Leser Black-backed Gull

Terns

Sandwich Tern *Sterna sandvicensis*

DATE   LOCATION

Elegant Tern *Sterna elegans*

DATE   LOCATION

Royal Tern *Sterna maxima*

DATE   LOCATION

Caspian Tern *Sterna caspia*

DATE   LOCATION

Sandwich Tern

juvenile

winter adult

breeding adult

juvenile

Elegant Tern

winter adult

breeding adult

juvenile

Royal Tern

breeding adult

winter adult

juvenile

juvenile

Caspian Tern

winter adult

breeding

juvenile

Roseate Tern *Sterna dougallii*

DATE   LOCATION

Forster's Tern *Sterna forsteri*

DATE   LOCATION

Gull-billed Tern *Sterna nilotica*

DATE   LOCATION

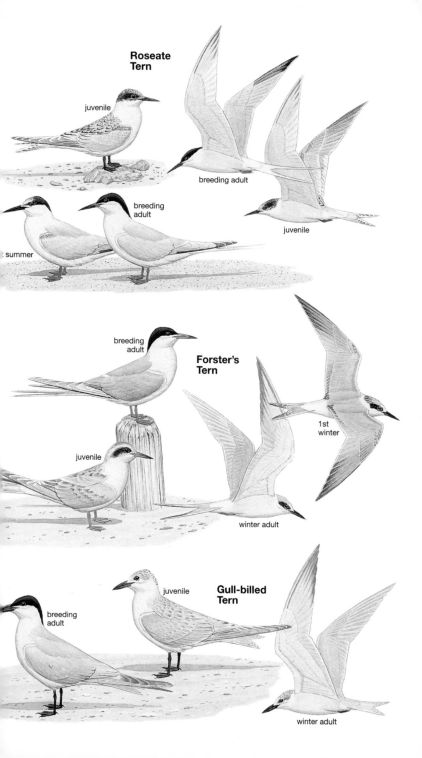

Roseate Tern

juvenile

breeding adult

breeding adult

summer

juvenile

Forster's Tern

breeding adult

juvenile

1st winter

winter adult

Gull-billed Tern

juvenile

breeding adult

winter adult

Common Tern *Sterna hirundo*

DATE   LOCATION

Arctic Tern *Sterna paradisaea*

DATE   LOCATION

Aleutian Tern *Sterna aleutica*

DATE   LOCATION

Common Tern

breeding adult

1st summer

juvenile

2nd summer

breeding adult *longipennis*

1st fall

breeding adult

juvenile

Arctic Tern

1st summer

breeding adult

breeding adult

juvenile

Aleutian Tern

juvenile

breeding adult

Least Tern *Sterna antillarum*

DATE   LOCATION

Black Tern *Chlidonias niger*

DATE   LOCATION

White-winged Tern *Chlidonias leucopterus*

DATE   LOCATION

Least Tern

breeding adult

juvenile

1st summer

breeding adult

Black Tern

breeding adult

1st summer

winter adult

breeding adult

juvenile

White-winged Tern

breeding adult

molting adult

winter adult

juvenile

Bridled Tern *Sterna anaethetus*

DATE   LOCATION

Sooty Tern *Sterna fuscata*

DATE   LOCATION

Black Noddy *Anous minutus*

DATE   LOCATION

Brown Noddy *Anous stolidus*

DATE   LOCATION

Large-billed Tern *Phaetusa simplex*

DATE   LOCATION

Black Skimmer *Rynchops niger*

DATE   LOCATION

Bridled Tern

breeding adult

juvenile

Sooty Tern

juvenile

breeding adult

Black Noddy

adult

immature

Brown Noddy

adults

immature

Large-billed Tern

breeding adult

juvenile

winter adults

Black Skimmer

breeding adult

Auks, Murres, Puffins (Family Alcidae)

Dovekie *Alle alle*

DATE   LOCATION

Common Murre *Uria aalge*

DATE   LOCATION

Thick-billed Murre *Uria lomvia*

DATE   LOCATION

Razorbill *Alca torda*

DATE   LOCATION

Dovekie

breeding adult

winter

breeding adult

winter

bridled breeding adult

breeding adult

Common Murre

breeding adult

winter

juvenile

Thick-billed Murre

Pacific winter *arra*

Atlantic breeding adults *lomvia*

immature

breeding adult

Razorbill

winter adult

breeding adult

breeding adult

Black Guillemot *Cepphus grylle*

DATE   LOCATION

Pigeon Guillemot *Cepphus columba*

DATE   LOCATION

Long-billed Murrelet *Brachyramphus perdix*

DATE   LOCATION

Marbled Murrelet *Brachyramphus marmoratus*

DATE   LOCATION

Kittlitz's Murrelet *Brachyramphus brevirostris*

DATE   LOCATION

Black Guillemot
arcticus

juvenile

winter adult

winter adult

breeding adult

Pigeon Guillemot

winter adult

juvenile

breeding adult

winter adult

Long-billed Murrelet

breeding adult

winter

Marbled Murrelet

juvenile

breeding adult

winter

winter

breeding adult

Kittlitz's Murrelet

juvenile

breeding adult

winter

winter

breeding adult

Xantus's Murrelet *Synthliboramphus hypoleucus*

DATE   LOCATION

Craveri's Murrelet *Synthliboramphus craveri*

DATE   LOCATION

Ancient Murrelet *Synthliboramphus antiquus*

DATE   LOCATION

Cassin's Auklet *Ptychoramphus aleuticus*

DATE   LOCATION

Xantus's Murrelet

scrippsi

hypoleucus

scrippsi

Craveri's Murrelet

breeding adult

immature

Ancient Murrelet

breeding adult

winter adult

adults

Cassin's Auklet

Parakeet Auklet *Aethia psittacula*

DATE   LOCATION

Crested Auklet *Aethia cristatella*

DATE   LOCATION

Whiskered Auklet *Aethia pygmaea*

DATE   LOCATION

Least Auklet *Aethia pusilla*

DATE   LOCATION

Parakeet Auklet

breeding adult

breeding adult

winter adult

Crested Auklet

breeding adult

juvenile

winter adult

breeding adult

Whiskered Auklet

breeding adult

breeding adult

juvenile

winter adult

Least Auklet

breeding adults

winter adults

juvenile

Rhinoceros Auklet *Cerorhinca monocerata*

DATE   LOCATION

Atlantic Puffin *Fratercula arctica*

DATE   LOCATION

Horned Puffin *Fratercula corniculata*

DATE   LOCATION

Tufted Puffin *Fratercula cirrhata*

DATE   LOCATION

Rhinoceros Auklet

winter adult

immature

winter adult

breeding adult

breeding adult

Atlantic Puffin

breeding adult

winter adult

juvenile

Horned Puffin

juvenile

winter adult

breeding adult

juvenile

juvenile

Tufted Puffin

winter adult

breeding adult

Pigeons and Doves (Family Columbidae)

Band-tailed Pigeon *Columba fasciata*

DATE .... LOCATION ....

....

....

....

....

Red-billed Pigeon *Columba flavirostris*

DATE .... LOCATION ....

....

....

....

....

White-crowned Pigeon *Columba leucocephala*

DATE .... LOCATION ....

....

....

....

....

Rock Dove *Columba livia*

DATE .... LOCATION ....

....

....

....

....

Band-tailed Pigeon

Red-billed Pigeon

White-crowned Pigeon

♂

♀

Rock Dove

color variations

Zenaida Dove *Zenaida aurita*

DATE   LOCATION

Mourning Dove *Zenaida macroura*

DATE   LOCATION

Spotted Dove *Streptopelia chinensis*

DATE   LOCATION

Eurasian Collared-Dove *Streptopelia decaocto*

DATE   LOCATION

White-winged Dove *Zenaida asiatica*

DATE   LOCATION

Oriental Turtle-Dove *Streptopelia orientalis*

DATE   LOCATION

Zenaida Dove

Eurasian Collared

Ringed Turtle

Spotted

Mourning

Mourning Dove

♂ ♀

juvenile

Spotted Dove

Ringed Turtle-Dove

Eurasian Collared-Dove

venile

White-winged Dove

Oriental Turtle-Dove *orientalis*

Common Ground-Dove *Columbina passerina*

DATE   LOCATION

Ruddy Ground-Dove *Columbina talpacoti*

DATE   LOCATION

Inca Dove *Columbina inca*

DATE   LOCATION

White-tipped Dove *Leptotila verreauxi*

DATE   LOCATION

Key West Quail-Dove *Geotrygon chrysia*

DATE   LOCATION

Ruddy Quail-Dove *Geotrygon montana*

DATE   LOCATION

Common Ground-Dove ♂ ♀ ♂ ♂

Ruddy Ground-Dove *eluta* ♀ ♂ ♂

Inca Dove

White-tipped Dove

Key West Quail-Dove ♂

Ruddy Quail-Dove ♀ ♂

Parakeets, Parrots (Family Psittacidae)

White-winged Parakeet *Brotogeris versicolurus*

DATE   LOCATION

Yellow-chevroned Parakeet *Brotogeris chiriri*

DATE   LOCATION

Monk Parakeet *Myiopsitta monachus*

DATE   LOCATION

Dusky-headed Parakeet *Aratinga weddelli*

DATE   LOCATION

Black-hooded Parakeet *Nandayus nenday*

DATE   LOCATION

Green Parakeet *Aratinga holochlora*

DATE   LOCATION

Blue-crowned Parakeet *Aratinga acuticaudata*

DATE   LOCATION

Mitred Parakeet *Aratinga mitrata*

DATE   LOCATION

Red-masked Parakeet *Aratinga erythrogenys*

DATE   LOCATION

White-winged Parakeet

Yellow-chevroned Parakeet

Monk Parakeet

Black-hooded Parakeet

Dusky-headed Parakeet

Green Parakeet

Blue-crowned Parakeet

Mitred Parakeet

Red-masked Parakeet

Thick-billed Parrot *Rhynchopsitta pachyrhyncha*

DATE   LOCATION

Rose-ringed Parakeet *Psittacula krameri*

DATE   LOCATION

Red-crowned Parrot *Amazona viridigenalis*

DATE   LOCATION

Orange-winged Parrot *Amazona amazonica*

DATE   LOCATION

Lilac-crowned Parrot *Amazona finschi*

DATE   LOCATION

Yellow-headed Parrot *Amazona oratrix*

DATE   LOCATION

Budgerigar *Melopsittacus undulatus*

DATE   LOCATION

Thick-billed Parrot

adult

Rose-ringed Parakeet

♂

♀

♂

Red-crowned Parrot

adult ♂

Orange-winged Parrot

Lilac-crowned Parrot

Budgerigar variants

Budgerigar

adults

Yellow-headed Parrot

Cuckoos, Roadrunners, Anis (Family Cuculidae)

Mangrove Cuckoo *Coccyzus minor*

DATE   LOCATION

Yellow-billed Cuckoo *Coccyzus americanus*

DATE   LOCATION

Black-billed Cuckoo *Coccyzus erythropthalmus*

DATE   LOCATION

Greater Roadrunner *Geococcyx californianus*

DATE   LOCATION

continentalis

maynardi

**Mangrove
Cuckoo**

**Yellow-billed
Cuckoo**

juvenile

**ack-billed
uckoo**

juvenile

**Greater
Roadrunner**

Common Cuckoo *Cuculus canorus*

DATE   LOCATION

Oriental Cuckoo *Cuculus saturatus*

DATE   LOCATION

Smooth-billed Ani *Crotophaga ani*

DATE   LOCATION

Groove-billed Ani *Crotophaga sulcirostris*

DATE   LOCATION

Common Cuckoo

hepatic morph ♀

hepatic morph ♀

♂

hepatic morph ♀

♂

sunning

hepatic morph ♀

Oriental Cuckoo

Smooth-billed Ani

Groove-billed Ani

Owls (Families Tytonidae and Strigidae)

Barn Owl *Tyto alba*

DATE   LOCATION

Short-eared Owl *Asio flammeus*

DATE   LOCATION

Long-eared Owl *Asio otus*

DATE   LOCATION

Great Horned Owl *Bubo virginianus*

DATE   LOCATION

Barn Owl

♂

♀

Long-eared Owl

Short-eared Owl

Great Horned Owl

subarcticus

Barred Owl *Strix varia*

DATE   LOCATION

Great Gray Owl *Strix nebulosa*

DATE   LOCATION

Spotted Owl *Strix occidentalis*

DATE   LOCATION

Snowy Owl *Nyctea scandiaca*

DATE   LOCATION

Barred Owl

Great Gray Owl

Spotted Owl

Snowy Owl

immature

Eastern Screech-Owl *Otus asio*

DATE   LOCATION

Western Screech-Owl *Otus kennicottii*

DATE   LOCATION

Whiskered Screech-Owl *Otus trichopsis*

DATE   LOCATION

Eastern Screech-Owl

red morph

gray morph

gray morph juvenile

maxwelliae

northwest coast *kennicottii*

Western Screech-Owl

Whiskered Screech-Owl

Flammulated Owl *Otus flammeolus*

DATE   LOCATION

Ferruginous Pygmy-Owl *Glaucidium brasilianum*

DATE   LOCATION

Elf Owl *Micrathene whitneyi*

DATE   LOCATION

Northern Pygmy-Owl *Glaucidium gnoma*

DATE   LOCATION

reddish type

Flammulated Owl

grayish type

Ferruginous Pygmy-Owl

Elf Owl

Northern Pygmy-Owl

Rockies type

Pacific coast type

Northern Saw-whet Owl *Aegolius acadicus*

DATE   LOCATION

Northern Hawk Owl *Surnia ulula*

DATE   LOCATION

Boreal Owl *Aegolius funereus*

DATE   LOCATION

Burrowing Owl *Athene cunicularia*

DATE   LOCATION

Northern Saw-whet Owl

juvenile

Northern Hawk Owl

Boreal Owl

juvenile

Burrowing Owl
western *hypugaea*

juvenile

Nighthawks, Nightjars (Family Caprimulgidae)

Lesser Nighthawk *Chordeiles acutipennis*

DATE   LOCATION

Common Nighthawk *Chordeiles minor*

DATE   LOCATION

Antillean Nighthawk *Chordeiles gundlachii*

DATE   LOCATION

Common Pauraque *Nyctidromus albicollis*

DATE   LOCATION

Lesser Nighthawk

Common Nighthawk

juvenile
henryi

Antillean Nighthawk

Common Pauraque

Chuck-will's-widow *Caprimulgus carolinensis*

DATE .... LOCATION ....

....

....

....

....

....

....

Whip-poor-will *Caprimulgus vociferus*

DATE .... LOCATION ....

....

....

....

....

....

Buff-collared Nightjar *Caprimulgus ridgwayi*

DATE .... LOCATION ....

....

....

....

....

....

Common Poorwill *Phalaenoptilus nuttallii*

DATE .... LOCATION ....

....

....

....

....

....

Chuck-will's-widow

Whip-poor-will
eastern *vociferus*

♀

vociferus ♀

vociferus ♂

southwestern
arizonae ♂

♂

**Buff-collared
Nightjar**

**Common
Poorwill**

♂

Swifts (Family Apodidae)

Black Swift *Cypseloides niger*

DATE   LOCATION

Vaux's Swift *Chaetura vauxi*

DATE   LOCATION

Chimney Swift *Chaetura pelagica*

DATE   LOCATION

Common Swift *Apus apus*

DATE   LOCATION

White-collared Swift *Streptoprocne zonaris*

DATE   LOCATION

White-throated Swift *Aeronautes saxatalis*

DATE   LOCATION

White-throated Needletail *Hirundapus caudacutus*

DATE   LOCATION

Fork-tailed Swift *Apus pacificus*

DATE   LOCATION

Black
Swift

juvenile

Vaux's
Swift

Chimney
Swift

White-collared
Swift

White-throated
Swift

Common
Swift

soaring

immature

soaring

Fork-tailed
Swift

White-throated
Needletail

Hummingbirds (Family Trochilidae)

Green Violet-ear *Colibri thalassinus*

DATE   LOCATION

Green-breasted Mango *Anthracothorax prevostii*

DATE   LOCATION

Buff-bellied Hummingbird *Amazilia yucatanensis*

DATE   LOCATION

Berylline Hummingbird *Amazilia beryllina*

DATE   LOCATION

Bahama Woodstar *Calliphlox evelynae*

DATE   LOCATION

Violet-crowned Hummingbird *Amazilia violiceps*

DATE   LOCATION

Lucifer Hummingbird *Calothorax lucifer*

DATE   LOCATION

immature

Green-breasted Mango

immature

♂

♀

♂

Green Violet-ear

♂

Buff-bellied Hummingbird

Berylline Hummingbird

♂

♀

♂

♂

immature ♂

Bahama Woodstar

♀

♀

♂

♀

Lucifer Hummingbird

♀

Violet-crowned Hummingbird

immature ♂

Broad-billed Hummingbird *Cynanthus latirostris*

DATE   LOCATION

White-eared Hummingbird *Hylocharis leucotis*

DATE   LOCATION

Blue-throated Hummingbird *Lampornis clemenciae*

DATE   LOCATION

Xantus's Hummingbird *Hylocharis xantusii*

DATE   LOCATION

Magnificent Hummingbird *Eugenes fulgens*

DATE   LOCATION

Plain-capped Starthroat *Heliomaster constantii*

DATE   LOCATION

Broad-billed Hummingbird

♀

immature ♂

♂

♂

White-eared Hummingbird

♀

♂

♂

Blue-throated Hummingbird

♀

♂

♂

♀

Xantus's Hummingbird

♀

Magnificent Hummingbird

♂

Plain-capped Starthroat

Ruby-throated Hummingbird *Archilochus colubris*

DATE   LOCATION

Black-chinned Hummingbird *Archilochus alexandri*

DATE   LOCATION

Costa's Hummingbird *Calypte costae*

DATE   LOCATION

Anna's Hummingbird *Calypte anna*

DATE   LOCATION

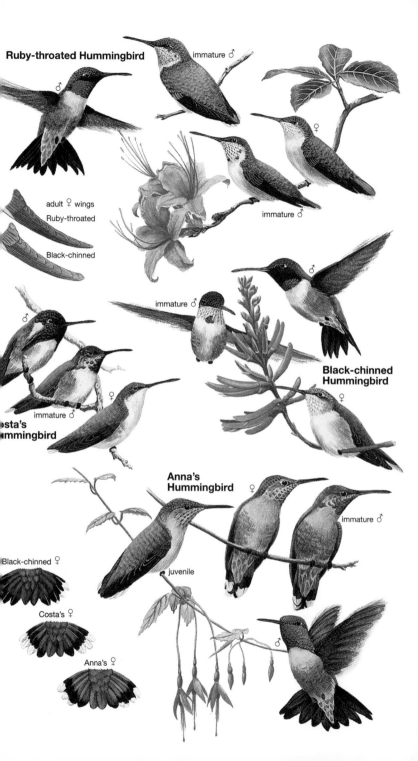

Ruby-throated Hummingbird

immature ♂

♂

♀

adult ♀ wings
Ruby-throated

Black-chinned

immature ♂

immature ♂

immature ♂

♂

♀

Black-chinned Hummingbird

♀

osta's
mmingbird

immature ♂

Anna's Hummingbird

♀

immature ♂

Black-chinned ♀

Costa's ♀

Anna's ♀

juvenile

♂

Broad-tailed Hummingbird *Selasphorus platycercus*

DATE   LOCATION

Calliope Hummingbird *Stellula calliope*

DATE   LOCATION

Rufous Hummingbird *Selasphorus rufus*

DATE   LOCATION

Allen's Hummingbird *Selasphorus sasin*

DATE   LOCATION

Trogons (Family Trogonidae)

Elegant Trogon *Trogon elegans*

DATE   LOCATION

Eared Trogon *Euptilotis neoxenus*

DATE   LOCATION

Broad-tailed Hummingbird

♂

♀

Calliope Hummingbird

♀

♂

Rufous Hummingbird

♀

♂

immature ♂

green-flecked ♂

Allen's Hummingbird

♂

Broad-tailed ♀ Rufous ♀ Allen's ♀ Calliope ♀

Elegant Trogan

♀

♂

Eared Trogon

♂

♀

♂ ♀

Kingfishers (Family Alcedinidae)

Belted Kingfisher *Ceryle alcyon*

DATE   LOCATION

Ringed Kingfisher *Ceryle torquata*

DATE   LOCATION

Green Kingfisher *Chloroceryle americana*

DATE   LOCATION

Belted Kingfisher

♀

♂

♂

Ringed Kingfisher

♂

♀

♂ **Green**

♀ **Kingfisher**

Woodpeckers (Family Picidae)

Red-headed Woodpecker *Melanerpes erythrocephalus*

DATE   LOCATION

Acorn Woodpecker *Melanerpes formicivorus*

DATE   LOCATION

White-headed Woodpecker *Picoides albolarvatus*

DATE   LOCATION

Lewis's Woodpecker *Melanerpes lewis*

DATE   LOCATION

Red-headed Woodpecker

juvenile

adults

Acorn Woodpecker

♂

♀

♂

White-headed Woodpecker

♂

♀

juvenile

Lewis's Woodpecker

adults

Golden-fronted Woodpecker *Melanerpes aurifrons*

DATE   LOCATION

Red-bellied Woodpecker *Melanerpes carolinus*

DATE   LOCATION

Gila Woodpecker *Melanerpes uropygialis*

DATE   LOCATION

Northern Flicker *Colaptes auratus*

DATE   LOCATION

Gilded Flicker *Colaptes chrysoides*

DATE   LOCATION

Golden-fronted Woodpecker

Red-bellied Woodpecker

Gila Woodpecker

"Yellow-shafted" ♂

Northern Flicker

"Red-shafted" ♂

"Yellow-shafted" ♂

Gilded Flicker

Gilded Flicker ♂

"Red-shafted" ♂

Sapsuckers

Williamson's Sapsucker *Sphyrapicus thyroideus*

DATE   LOCATION

Red-breasted Sapsucker *Sphyrapicus ruber*

DATE   LOCATION

Yellow-bellied Sapsucker *Sphyrapicus varius*

DATE   LOCATION

Red-naped Sapsucker *Sphyrapicus nuchalis*

DATE   LOCATION

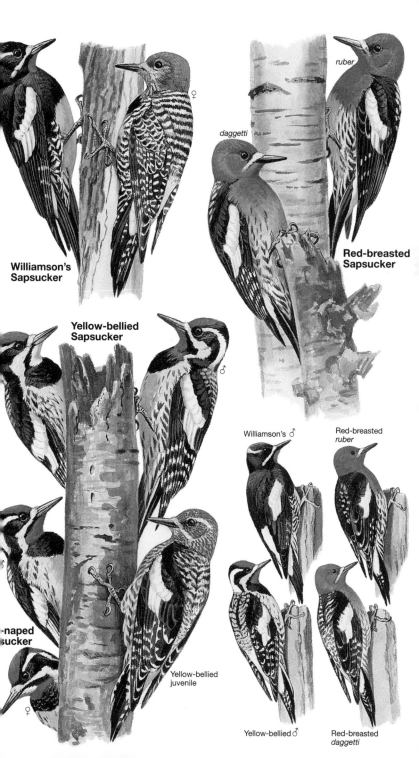

Williamson's Sapsucker

♀

ruber

daggetti

Red-breasted Sapsucker

Yellow-bellied Sapsucker

♂

-naped sucker

♀

Yellow-bellied juvenile

Williamson's ♂

Red-breasted *ruber*

Yellow-bellied ♂

Red-breasted *daggetti*

Ladder-backed Woodpecker *Picoides scalaris*

DATE   LOCATION

Red-cockaded Woodpecker *Picoides borealis*

DATE   LOCATION

Nuttall's Woodpecker *Picoides nuttallii*

DATE   LOCATION

Strickland's Woodpecker *Picoides stricklandi*

DATE   LOCATION

adder-backed
Woodpecker

Red-cockaded
Woodpecker

Nuttall's
Woodpecker

Strickland's
Woodpecker

dder-backed ♂   Nuttall's ♂   Strickland's ♂   Red-cockaded ♂

Downy Woodpecker *Picoides pubescens*

DATE   LOCATION

Hairy Woodpecker *Picoides villosus*

DATE   LOCATION

Three-toed Woodpecker *Picoides tridactylus*

DATE   LOCATION

Black-backed Woodpecker *Picoides arcticus*

DATE   LOCATION

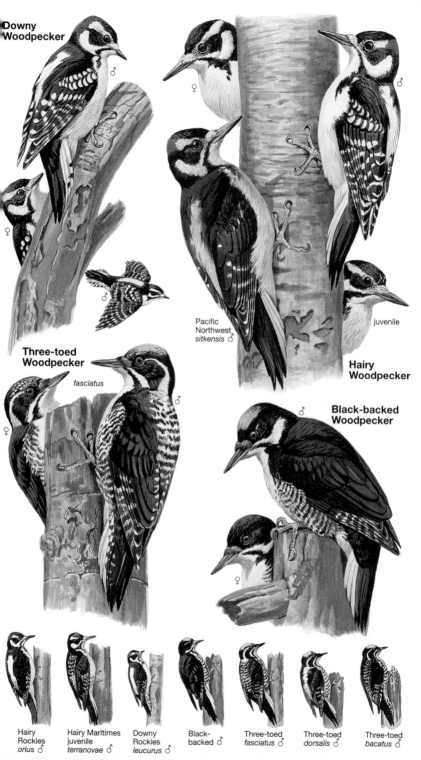

Downy Woodpecker

♂

♀

♀

♂

Three-toed Woodpecker

fasciatus

♀

♂

Pacific Northwest *sitkensis* ♂

Hairy Woodpecker

juvenile

Black-backed Woodpecker

♂

♀

Hairy Rockies *orius* ♂

Hairy Maritimes juvenile *terranovae* ♂

Downy Rockies *leucurus* ♂

Black-backed ♂

Three-toed *fasciatus* ♂

Three-toed *dorsalis* ♂

Three-toed *bacatus* ♂

Ivory-billed Woodpecker *Campephilus principalis*

DATE   LOCATION

Pileated Woodpecker *Dryocopus pileatus*

DATE   LOCATION

Ivory-billed Woodpecker

Pileated Woodpecker

Tyrant Flycatchers (Family Tyrannidae)

Greater Pewee *Contopus pertinax*

DATE   LOCATION

Olive-sided Flycatcher *Contopus cooperi*

DATE   LOCATION

Eastern Wood-Pewee *Contopus virens*

DATE   LOCATION

Western Wood-Pewee *Contopus sordidulus*

DATE   LOCATION

Cuban Pewee *Contopus caribaeus*

DATE   LOCATION

Greater
Pewee

Olive-sided
Flycatcher

winter

summer

immature

juvenile

Eastern
Wood-
Pewee

Western
Wood-
Pewee

Cuban
Pewee

Empidonax Flycatchers

Acadian Flycatcher *Empidonax virescens*

DATE   LOCATION

Yellow-bellied Flycatcher *Empidonax flaviventris*

DATE   LOCATION

Alder Flycatcher *Empidonax alnorum*

DATE   LOCATION

Willow Flycatcher *Empidonax traillii*

DATE   LOCATION

Acadian Flycatcher

worn summer adult

spring

1st fall

Yellow-bellied Flycatcher

worn fall adult

spring

Alder Flycatcher

worn fall adult

1st fall

spring

Willow Flycatcher

spring *extimus*

spring *brewsteri*

1st fall *traillii*

worn fall adult *traillii*

spring *traillii*

Least Flycatcher *Empidonax minimus*

DATE   LOCATION

Hammond's Flycatcher *Empidonax hammondii*

DATE   LOCATION

Gray Flycatcher *Empidonax wrightii*

DATE   LOCATION

Dusky Flycatcher *Empidonax oberholseri*

DATE   LOCATION

Least Flycatcher

1st fall

worn fall adult

spring

Hammond's Flycatcher

fall

spring

Gray Flycatcher

winter

spring

Dusky Flycatcher

1st fall

worn fall adult

winter

spring

Pacific-slope Flycatcher *Empidonax difficilis*

DATE   LOCATION

Cordilleran Flycatcher *Empidonax occidentalis*

DATE   LOCATION

Buff-breasted Flycatcher *Empidonax fulvifrons*

DATE   LOCATION

Northern Beardless-Tyrannulet *Camptostoma imberbe*

DATE   LOCATION

Pacific-slope Flycatcher

pale 1st fall

1st fall

worn fall adult

spring

spring

Yellow-bellied Flycatcher for comparison

Cordilleran Flycatcher

spring

worn summer adult

Buff-breasted Flycatcher

fresh

Northern Beardless-Tyrannulet

worn adult

fresh

Eastern Phoebe *Sayornis phoebe*

DATE   LOCATION

Black Phoebe *Sayornis nigricans*

DATE   LOCATION

Say's Phoebe *Sayornis saya*

DATE   LOCATION

Vermilion Flycatcher *Pyrocephalus rubinus*

DATE   LOCATION

Eastern Phoebe

worn summer adult

fresh fall

Black Phoebe

juvenile

Say's Phoebe

immature ♀

Vermilion Flycatcher

immature ♂

♀

adult ♂

juvenile

Brown-crested Flycatcher *Myiarchus tyrannulus*

DATE   LOCATION

Great Crested Flycatcher *Myiarchus crinitus*

DATE   LOCATION

Nutting's Flycatcher *Myiarchus nuttingi*

DATE   LOCATION

Ash-throated Flycatcher *Myiarchus cinerascens*

DATE   LOCATION

La Sagra's Flycatcher *Myiarchus sagrae*

DATE   LOCATION

Dusky-capped Flycatcher *Myiarchus tuberculifer*

DATE   LOCATION

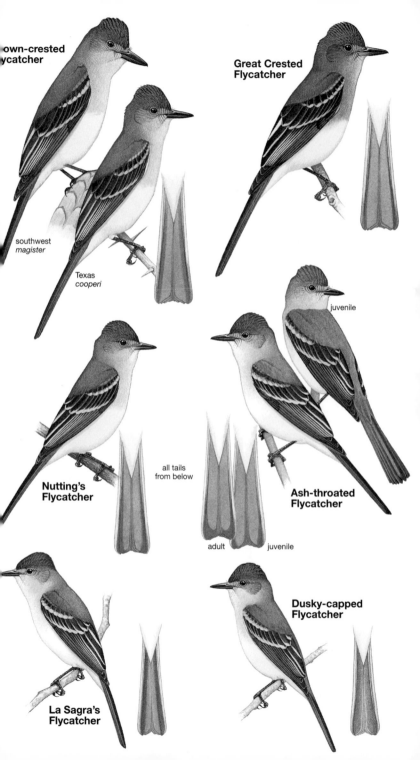

Brown-crested
Flycatcher

Great Crested
Flycatcher

southwest
magister

Texas
cooperi

juvenile

Nutting's
Flycatcher

all tails
from below

Ash-throated
Flycatcher

adult   juvenile

La Sagra's
Flycatcher

Dusky-capped
Flycatcher

Western Kingbird *Tyrannus verticalis*

DATE   LOCATION

Cassin's Kingbird *Tyrannus vociferans*

DATE   LOCATION

Tropical Kingbird *Tyrannus melancholicus*

DATE   LOCATION

Couch's Kingbird *Tyrannus couchii*

DATE   LOCATION

Western Kingbird

Cassin's Kingbird

Tropical Kingbird

Couch's Kingbird

tails from above

Western

Cassin's

Couch's

Tropical

Fork-tailed Flycatcher *Tyrannus savana*

DATE   LOCATION

....

....

....

....

Eastern Kingbird *Tyrannus tyrannus*

DATE   LOCATION

....

....

....

....

Loggerhead Kingbird *Tyrannus caudifasciatus*

DATE   LOCATION

....

....

....

....

Gray Kingbird *Tyrannus dominicensis*

DATE   LOCATION

....

....

....

....

Thick-billed Kingbird *Tyrannus crassirostris*

DATE   LOCATION

....

....

....

Fork-tailed Flycatcher

adult

Eastern Kingbird

juvenile

Loggerhead Kingbird

Gray Kingbird

1st fall

Thick-billed Kingbird

worn summer adult

Scissor-tailed Flycatcher *Tyrannus forficatus*

DATE   LOCATION

Piratic Flycatcher *Legatus leucophaius*

DATE   LOCATION

Variegated Flycatcher *Empidonomus varius*

DATE   LOCATION

Great Kiskadee *Pitangus sulphuratus*

DATE   LOCATION

Sulphur-bellied Flycatcher *Myiodynastes luteiventris*

DATE   LOCATION

Rose-throated Becard *Pachyramphus aglaiae*

DATE   LOCATION

Scissor-tailed Flycatcher

juvenile

juvenile

♂

Piratic Flycatcher
variegatus

Great Kiskadee

Variegated Flycatcher
varius

Rose-throated Becard
albiventris

♂

Sulphur-bellied Flycatcher

1st fall ♂

♀

Shrikes (Family Laniidae)

Brown Shrike *Lanius cristatus*

DATE   LOCATION

Loggerhead Shrike *Lanius ludovicianus*

DATE   LOCATION

Northern Shrike *Lanius excubitor*

DATE   LOCATION

Brown Shrike
cristatus

♀

juvenile

♂

juvenile

Loggerhead Shrike

Northern Mockingbird for comparison

Northern Shrike

adult

immature

juvenile

Vireos (Family Vireonidae)

Black-capped Vireo *Vireo atricapillus*

DATE LOCATION

White-eyed Vireo *Vireo griseus*

DATE LOCATION

Thick-billed Vireo *Vireo crassirostris*

DATE LOCATION

Yellow-throated Vireo *Vireo flavifrons*

DATE LOCATION

Black-capped Vireo

adult ♀

adult ♂

immature ♀

White-eyed Vireo

Florida Keys
maynardi

Yellow-throated Vireo

Thick-billed Vireo
crassirostris

adult ♂ Pine Warbler
for comparison

Bell's Vireo *Vireo bellii*

DATE   LOCATION

Hutton's Vireo *Vireo huttoni*

DATE   LOCATION

Gray Vireo *Vireo vicinior*

DATE   LOCATION

Blue-headed Vireo *Vireo solitarius*

DATE   LOCATION

Plumbeous Vireo *Vireo plumbeus*

DATE   LOCATION

Cassin's Vireo *Vireo cassinii*

DATE   LOCATION

Ruby-crowned Kinglet
for comparison

bellii

Bell's
Vireo

west coast
pusillus

Hutton's
Vireo

west coast
huttoni

southwest
stephensi

Gray Vireo

Blue-headed
Vireo

solitarius ♂

Plumbeous
Vireo

Cassin's
Vireo   ♀

Yellow-green Vireo *Vireo flavoviridis*

DATE   LOCATION

Red-eyed Vireo *Vireo olivaceus*

DATE   LOCATION

Black-whiskered Vireo *Vireo altiloquus*

DATE   LOCATION

Philadelphia Vireo *Vireo philadelphicus*

DATE   LOCATION

Warbling Vireo *Vireo gilvus*

DATE   LOCATION

Yellow-green Vireo

breeding

Red-eyed Vireo

1st fall

Black-whiskered Vireo

Florida *barbatulus*

Philadelphia Vireo

fall

spring

spring *gilvus*

fall *gilvus*

Warbling Vireo

fall *swainsoni*

Crows, Jays (Family Corvidae)

Blue Jay *Cyanocitta cristata*

DATE   LOCATION

Steller's Jay *Cyanocitta stelleri*

DATE   LOCATION

Gray Jay *Perisoreus canadensis*

DATE   LOCATION

Clark's Nutcracker *Nucifraga columbiana*

DATE   LOCATION

Blue Jay

Steller's Jay

stelleri

southern Rockies *macrolopha*

Gray Jay

juvenile

boreal *canadensis*

southern Rockies *capitalis*

northwest *obscurus*

Clark's Nutcracker

Western Scrub-Jay *Aphelocoma californica*

DATE   LOCATION

Island Scrub-Jay *Aphelocoma insularis*

DATE   LOCATION

Florida Scrub-Jay *Aphelocoma coerulescens*

DATE   LOCATION

Mexican Jay *Aphelocoma ultramarina*

DATE   LOCATION

Pinyon Jay *Gymnorhinus cyanocephalus*

DATE   LOCATION

interior juvenile
woodhouseii

**Western
Scrub-Jay**

interior
woodhouseii

coastal
californica

**Island
Scrub-Jay**

**Florida
Scrub-Jay**

**Mexican
Jay**

Arizona
arizonae

Texas
couchii

**Pinyon
Jay**

juvenile
arizonae

Brown Jay *Cyanocorax morio*

DATE   LOCATION

Green Jay *Cyanocorax yncas*

DATE   LOCATION

Black-billed Magpie *Pica pica*

DATE   LOCATION

Yellow-billed Magpie *Pica nuttalli*

DATE   LOCATION

juvenile

Brown Jay

Green Jay

Black-billed Magpie

Yellow-billed Magpie

Eurasian Jackdaw *Corvus monedula*

DATE   LOCATION

Tamaulipas Crow *Corvus imparatus*

DATE   LOCATION

American Crow *Corvus brachyrhynchos*

DATE   LOCATION

Northwestern Crow *Corvus caurinus*

DATE   LOCATION

Fish Crow *Corvus ossifragus*

DATE   LOCATION

Chihuahuan Raven *Corvus cryptoleucus*

DATE   LOCATION

Common Raven *Corvus corax*

DATE   LOCATION

Eurasian
Jackdaw

Tamaulipas
Crow

American
Crow

Chihuahuan
Raven

Fish
Crow

Common
Raven

Larks (Family Alaudidae)

Sky Lark *Alauda arvensis*

DATE............................LOCATION...

....

....

....

....

....

....

....

....

....

....

....

Horned Lark *Eremophila alpestris*

DATE............................LOCATION...

....

....

....

....

....

....

....

....

....

....

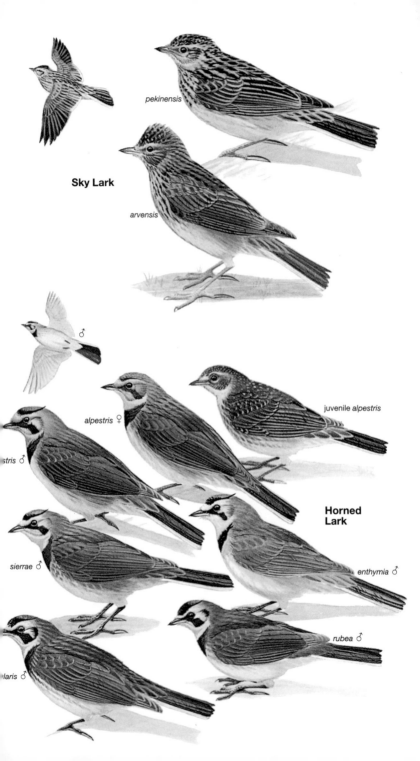

Sky Lark

pekinensis

arvensis

♂

alpestris ♀

juvenile *alpestris*

...stris ♂

Horned Lark

sierrae ♂

enthymia ♂

...laris ♂

rubea ♂

Swallows (Family Hirundinidae)

Tree Swallow *Tachycineta bicolor*

DATE   LOCATION

Bahama Swallow *Tachycineta cyaneoviridis*

DATE   LOCATION

Violet-green Swallow *Tachycineta thalassina*

DATE   LOCATION

Purple Martin *Progne subis*

DATE   LOCATION

Common House-Martin *Delichon urbica*

DATE   LOCATION

**Tree
Swallow**

spring adult ♀

1st spring ♀

juvenile

juvenile

fall adult ♂

spring ♂

**Bahama
Swallow**

adults

♂
adults

juvenile

**Violet-green
Swallow**

adult ♂

**Common
House-Martin**
lagopoda

**Purple
Martin**

♀

adult ♂

1st spring ♂

♀

adult ♂

Bank Swallow *Riparia riparia*

DATE   LOCATION

Cliff Swallow *Petrochelidon pyrrhonota*

DATE   LOCATION

Northern Rough-winged Swallow *Stelgidopteryx serripennis*

DATE   LOCATION

Barn Swallow *Hirundo rustica*

DATE   LOCATION

Cave Swallow *Petrochelidon fulva*

DATE   LOCATION

Bank Swallow

juvenile

southwestern
melanogaster

**Northern
Rough-winged
Swallow**

juvenile

juvenile

**Cliff
Swallow**

juvenile

Eurasian
rustica

juvenile

southwest
pelodoma

dark

juvenile

**Barn
Swallow**

**Cave
Swallow**

West
Indies
fulva

Babblers (Family Timaliidae)

Wrentit *Chamaea fasciata*

DATE   LOCATION

Chickadees, Titmice (Family Paridae)

Bridled Titmouse *Baeolophus wollweberi*

DATE   LOCATION

Oak Titmouse *Baeolophus inornatus*

DATE   LOCATION

Juniper Titmouse *Baeolophus griseus*

DATE   LOCATION

Tufted Titmouse *Baeolophus bicolor*

DATE   LOCATION

northern

southern

Wrentit

Bridled Titmouse

Oak Titmouse
affabilis

Juniper Titmouse

Tufted Titmouse

"Black-crested Titmouse"

Black-capped Chickadee *Poecile atricapillus*

DATE   LOCATION

Carolina Chickadee *Poecile carolinensis*

DATE   LOCATION

Mexican Chickadee *Poecile sclateri*

DATE   LOCATION

Mountain Chickadee *Poecile gambeli*

DATE   LOCATION

fresh fall

Black-capped
Chickadee

worn summer

Carolina
Chickadee

Mexican
Chickadee

Mountain
Chickadee

Rockies *gambeli*

baileyae

Chestnut-backed Chickadee *Poecile rufescens*

DATE   LOCATION

Gray-headed Chickadee *Poecile cinctus*

DATE   LOCATION

Boreal Chickadee *Poecile hudsonicus*

DATE   LOCATION

Verdins (Family Remizidae)

Verdin *Auriparus flaviceps*

DATE   LOCATION

Bushtits (Family Aegithalidae)

Bushtit *Psaltriparus minimus*

DATE   LOCATION

rufescens

Chestnut-backed Chickadee

coastal central California
barlowi

Gray-headed Chickadee

Boreal Chickadee

Verdin

Bushtit

interior ♂
plumbeus

interior ♀
plumbeus

nile

"Black-eared Bushtit"
juvenile ♂

coastal ♂

Creepers (Family Certhiidae)

Brown Creeper *Certhia americana*

DATE   LOCATION

Nuthatches (Family Sittidae)

White-breasted Nuthatch *Sitta carolinensis*

DATE   LOCATION

Red-breasted Nuthatch *Sitta canadensis*

DATE   LOCATION

Pygmy Nuthatch *Sitta pygmaea*

DATE   LOCATION

Brown-headed Nuthatch *Sitta pusilla*

DATE   LOCATION

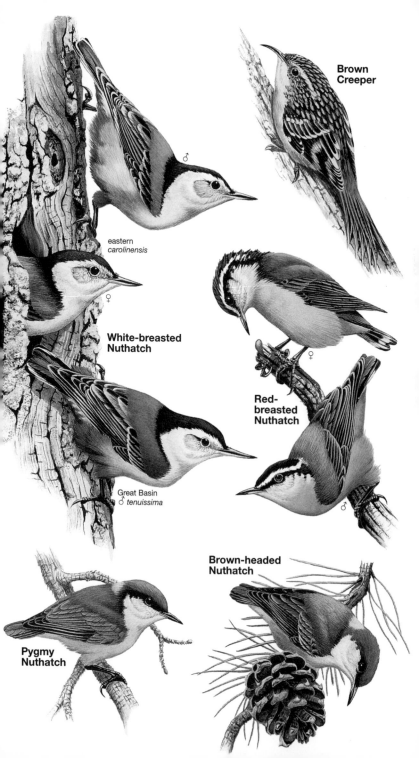

Brown Creeper

eastern
carolinensis

♂

♀

White-breasted Nuthatch

Red-breasted Nuthatch

♀

♂

Great Basin
♂ *tenuissima*

Pygmy Nuthatch

Brown-headed Nuthatch

Wrens (Family Troglodytidae)

House Wren *Troglodytes aedon*

DATE .... LOCATION ....

....

....

....

....

....

Winter Wren *Troglodytes troglodytes*

DATE .... LOCATION ....

....

....

....

....

....

Carolina Wren *Thryothorus ludovicianus*

DATE .... LOCATION ....

....

....

....

....

....

Bewick's Wren *Thryomanes bewickii*

DATE .... LOCATION ....

....

....

....

....

....

southeast Arizona
"Brown-throated Wren"

**House
Wren**

juvenile

western
parkmanii

eastern
aedon

Aleutians

western
pacificus

**Winter
Wren**

**Carolina
Wren**

eastern
hiemalis

western interior
eremophilus

eastern
bewickii

Bewick's Wren

Cactus Wren *Campylorhynchus brunneicapillus*

DATE   LOCATION

Rock Wren *Salpinctes obsoletus*

DATE   LOCATION

Canyon Wren *Catherpes mexicanus*

DATE   LOCATION

Marsh Wren *Cistothorus palustris*

DATE   LOCATION

Sedge Wren *Cistothorus platensis*

DATE   LOCATION

Dippers (Family Cinclidae)

American Dipper *Cinclus mexicanus*

DATE   LOCATION

Rock
Wren

Cactus
Wren

Canyon
Wren

Marsh
Wren

Sedge
Wren

juvenile

American
Dipper

Kinglets (Family Regulidae)

Golden-crowned Kinglet *Regulus satrapa*

DATE   LOCATION

Ruby-crowned Kinglet *Regulus calendula*

DATE   LOCATION

Old World Warblers, Gnatcatchers (Family Sylviidae)

Blue-gray Gnatcatcher *Polioptila caerulea*

DATE   LOCATION

Black-capped Gnatcatcher *Polioptila nigriceps*

DATE   LOCATION

Black-tailed Gnatcatcher *Polioptila melanura*

DATE   LOCATION

California Gnatcatcher *Polioptilla californica*

DATE   LOCATION

Golden-crowned Kinglet

♀

♂

Ruby-crowned Kinglet

♀

♂

♀

eding ♂

Blue-gray Gnatcatcher

♀

breeding ♂

Black-capped Gnatcatcher

breeding ♂

Black-tailed Gnatcatcher

♀

♀

California Gnatcatcher

breeding ♂

Lanceolated Warbler *Locustella lanceolata*

DATE   LOCATION

Middendorff's Grasshopper-Warbler *Locustella ochotensis*

DATE   LOCATION

Dusky Warbler *Phylloscopus fuscatus*

DATE   LOCATION

Arctic Warbler *Phylloscopus borealis*

DATE   LOCATION

Lanceolated Warbler

adult

Middendorff's Grasshopper-Warbler

spring

fall

Dusky Warbler

fall
kennicotti

spring
kennicotti

Arctic Warbler

borealis

Old World Flycatchers (Family Muscicapidae)

Narcissus Flycatcher *Ficedula narcissina*

DATE .... LOCATION ....

Siberian Flycatcher *Muscicapa sibirica*

DATE .... LOCATION ....

Red-breasted Flycatcher *Ficedula parva*

DATE .... LOCATION ....

Gray-spotted Flycatcher *Muscicapa griseisticta*

DATE .... LOCATION ....

Asian Brown Flycatcher *Muscicapa dauurica*

DATE .... LOCATION ....

Narcissus Flycatcher

adult ♂

1st spring ♂

spring ♀

♀

♀

breeding adult ♂

1st fall

Siberian Flycatcher

spring

1st fall

Red-breasted Flycatcher
albicilla

spring ♀

Gray-spotted Flycatcher

spring

1st fall

spring

Asian Brown Flycatcher

1st fall

Thrushes (Family Turdidae)

Siberian Rubythroat *Luscinia calliope*

DATE   LOCATION

Bluethroat *Luscinia svecica*

DATE   LOCATION

Red-flanked Bluetail *Tarsiger cyanurus*

DATE   LOCATION

Northern Wheatear *Oenanthe oenanthe*

DATE   LOCATION

Stonechat *Saxicola torquata*

DATE   LOCATION

Siberian Rubythroat

adult ♂

1st fall ♂

pink-throated adult ♀

♀

1st fall ♀

♀

Bluethroat

♀

breeding ♂

winter adult ♂

Red-flanked Bluetail

♀

adult ♂

spring ♀ *oenanthe*

breeding adult ♂ *oenanthe*

fall adult ♂ *oenanthe*

Northern Wheatear

♀

1st fall *leucorhoa*

breeding adult ♂ *leucorhoa*

1st fall

spring ♂

spring ♀

fall adult ♂

Stonechat
maura group

Eastern Bluebird *Sialia sialis*

DATE   LOCATION

....

....

....

....

....

....

Western Bluebird *Sialia mexicana*

DATE   LOCATION

....

....

....

....

....

Mountain Bluebird *Sialia currucoides*

DATE   LOCATION

....

....

....

....

....

Townsend's Solitaire *Myadestes townsendi*

DATE   LOCATION

....

....

....

....

....

Eastern Bluebird
sialis

juvenile

♀

♂

southwestern
♂ *fulva*

Western Bluebird

♀

♂

Mountain Bluebird

♀

♂

juvenile

Townsend's Solitaire

Wood Thrush *Hylocichla mustelina*

DATE   LOCATION

Veery *Catharus fuscescens*

DATE   LOCATION

Gray-cheeked Thrush *Catharus minimus*

DATE   LOCATION

Bicknell's Thrush *Catharus bicknelli*

DATE   LOCATION

Swainson's Thrush *Catharus ustulatus*

DATE   LOCATION

Hermit Thrush *Catharus guttatus*

DATE   LOCATION

Wood Thrush

Veery

western
salicicola

eastern
fuscescens

1st fall
aliciae

aliciae

Bicknell's Thrush

Gray-cheeked Thrush

minimus

cific coast
tulatus

Alaska
incanus

juvenile
faxoni

faxoni

Swainson's Thrush

wainsoni

Hermit Thrush

auduboni

guttatus

Varied Thrush *Ixoreus naevius*

DATE   LOCATION

Eyebrowed Thrush *Turdus obscurus*

DATE   LOCATION

Dusky Thrush *Turdus naumanni*

DATE   LOCATION

Fieldfare *Turdus pilaris*

DATE   LOCATION

Redwing *Turdus iliacus*

DATE   LOCATION

Varied Thrush

juvenile

♀

♂

Eyebrowed Thrush

♀

♂

Dusky Thrush

Fieldfare

Redwing

American Robin *Turdus migratorius*

DATE   LOCATION

White-throated Robin *Turdus assimilis*

DATE   LOCATION

Rufous-backed Robin *Turdus rufopalliatus*

DATE   LOCATION

Clay-colored Robin *Turdus grayi*

DATE   LOCATION

Aztec Thrush *Ridgwayia pinicola*

DATE   LOCATION

juvenile

American Robin

♀

♂

Rufous-backed Robin

White-throated Robin

Clay-colored Robin

juvenile

Aztec Thrush

♂

♀

Mockingbirds, Thrashers (Family Mimidae)

Gray Catbird *Dumetella carolinensis*

DATE   LOCATION

Northern Mockingbird *Mimus polyglottos*

DATE   LOCATION

Bahama Mockingbird *Mimus gundlachii*

DATE   LOCATION

Brown Thrasher *Toxostoma rufum*

DATE   LOCATION

Long-billed Thrasher *Toxostoma longirostre*

DATE   LOCATION

Gray
Catbird

juvenile

Northern
Mockingbird

Bahama
Mockingbird

Brown
Thrasher

Long-billed
Thrasher

Sage Thrasher *Oreoscoptes montanus*

DATE   LOCATION

....

....

....

....

Bendire's Thrasher *Toxostoma bendirei*

DATE   LOCATION

....

....

....

....

Curve-billed Thrasher *Toxostoma curvirostre*

DATE   LOCATION

....

....

....

....

California Thrasher *Toxostoma redivivum*

DATE   LOCATION

....

....

....

....

Crissal Thrasher *Toxostoma crissale*

DATE   LOCATION

....

....

....

....

Le Conte's Thrasher *Toxostoma lecontei*

DATE   LOCATION

....

....

....

Sage Thrasher

worn adult

Bendire's Thrasher

worn

fresh

juvenile *palmeri*

Curve-billed Thrasher

ndire's

Curve-billed
palmeri   *oberholseri*

oberholseri

palmeri

California Thrasher

Le Conte's Thrasher

Crissal Thrasher

Bulbuls (Family Pycnonotidae)

Red-whiskered Bulbul *Pycnonotus jocosus*

DATE................................LOCATION...

....

....

....

....

Starlings (Family Sturnidae)

Crested Myna *Acridotheres cristatellus*

DATE................................LOCATION...

....

....

....

Common Myna *Acridotheres tristis*

DATE................................LOCATION...

....

....

....

Hill Myna *Gracula religiosa*

DATE................................LOCATION...

....

....

....

European Starling *Sturnus vulgaris*

DATE................................LOCATION...

....

....

....

Red-whiskered Bulbul

juvenile

Crested Myna

Common Myna

Hill Myna

fall

European Starling

winter

breeding ♂

Brown-headed Cowbird for comparison

juvenile

Accentors (Family Prunellidae)

Siberian Accentor *Prunella montanella*

DATE   LOCATION

Wagtails, Pipits (Family Motacillidae)

Yellow Wagtail *Motacilla flava*

DATE   LOCATION

Gray Wagtail *Motacilla cinerea*

DATE   LOCATION

White Wagtail *Motacilla alba*

DATE   LOCATION

Black-backed Wagtail *Motacilla lugens*

DATE   LOCATION

Siberian Accentor

Yellow Wagtail
tschutschensis

breeding ♂

juvenile

immature

breeding ♂

Gray Wagtail

breeding ♂

♀

breeding ♂

breeding ♀

breeding ♂
simillima

White Wagtail

breeding

breeding
adult ♂

breeding
adult ♂

adult breeding ♀

winter adult ♂

immature

Black-backed Wagtail

American Pipit *Anthus rubescens*

DATE   LOCATION

Sprague's Pipit *Anthus spragueii*

DATE   LOCATION

Olive-backed Pipit *Anthus hodgsoni*

DATE   LOCATION

Pechora Pipit *Anthus gustavi*

DATE   LOCATION

Red-throated Pipit *Anthus cervinus*

DATE   LOCATION

American Pipit

breeding *rubescens*

winter *rubescens*

winter *japonicus*

Sprague's Pipit

Olive-backed Pipit

yunnanensis

Pechora Pipit

breeding ♀

Red-throated Pipit

immature

breeding ♂

Waxwings (Family Bombycillidae)

Bohemian Waxwing *Bombycilla garrulus*

DATE   LOCATION

Cedar Waxwing *Bombycilla cedrorum*

DATE   LOCATION

Silky-flycatchers (Family Ptilogonatidae)

Phainopepla *Phainopepla nitens*

DATE   LOCATION

juvenile

Bohemian Waxwing

juvenile

Cedar Waxwing

Phainopepla

♂

♀

♂

Wood-Warblers (Family Parulidae)

Prothonotary Warbler *Protonotaria citrea*

DATE   LOCATION

....

....

....

....

....

....

....

....

Blue-winged Warbler *Vermivora pinus*

DATE   LOCATION

....

....

....

....

....

....

....

....

Golden-winged Warbler *Vermivora chrysoptera*

DATE   LOCATION

....

....

....

....

....

....

....

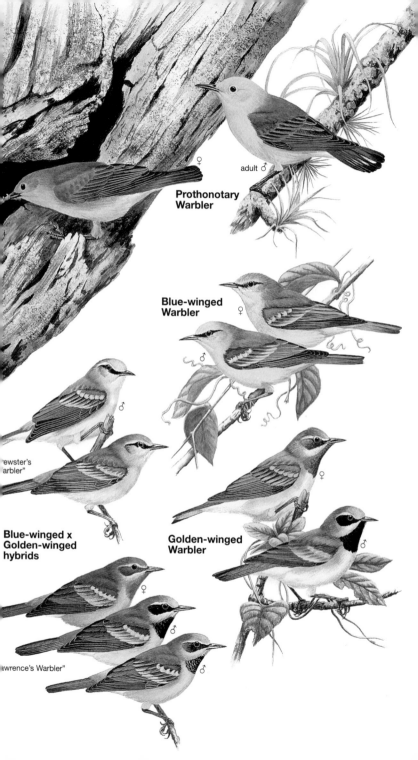

♀

adult ♂

Prothonotary Warbler

Blue-winged Warbler

♀

♂

"Brewster's Warbler"

Blue-winged x Golden-winged hybrids

Golden-winged Warbler

♀

♂

♂

"Lawrence's Warbler"

♂

Tennessee Warbler *Vermivora peregrina*

DATE   LOCATION

Orange-crowned Warbler *Vermivora celata*

DATE   LOCATION

Bachman's Warbler *Vermivora bachmanii*

DATE   LOCATION

fall

fall

breeding ♀

Tennessee Warbler

breeding ♂

♀

celata

♂

Orange-crowned Warbler

lutescens ♂

adult ♀

1st spring ♂

Bachman's Warbler

adult ♂

Nashville Warbler *Vermivora ruficapilla*

DATE   LOCATION

Virginia's Warbler *Vermivora virginiae*

DATE   LOCATION

Colima Warbler *Vermivora crissalis*

DATE   LOCATION

Lucy's Warbler *Vermivora luciae*

DATE   LOCATION

Crescent-chested Warbler *Parula superciliosa*

DATE   LOCATION

Northern Parula *Parula americana*

DATE   LOCATION

Tropical Parula *Parula pitiayumi*

DATE   LOCATION

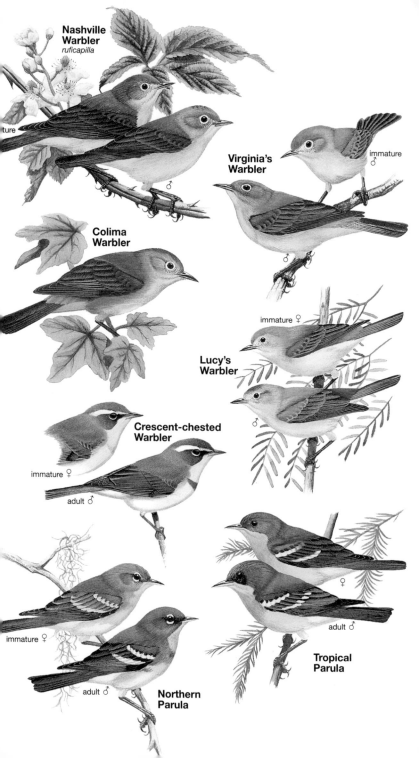

Nashville Warbler
ruficapilla

immature

Virginia's Warbler

immature ♂

♂

Colima Warbler

Lucy's Warbler

immature ♀

♂

Crescent-chested Warbler

immature ♀

adult ♂

Northern Parula

immature ♀

adult ♂

Tropical Parula

♀

adult ♂

Chestnut-sided Warbler *Dendroica pensylvanica*

DATE   LOCATION

Cape May Warbler *Dendroica tigrina*

DATE   LOCATION

Magnolia Warbler *Dendroica magnolia*

DATE   LOCATION

Yellow-rumped Warbler *Dendroica coronata*

DATE   LOCATION

Chestnut-sided Warbler

breeding adult ♀

breeding adult ♂

immature ♀

Magnolia Warbler

breeding ♀

breeding adult ♂

Cape May Warbler

1st spring ♀

immature ♀

breeding adult ♂

immature ♂

immature ♀

fall adult ♂

"Myrtle Warbler"

"Audubon's Warbler"

breeding ♀

southwest breeding ♂

breeding ♂

Yellow-rumped Warbler

fall ♀

fall ♀

breeding ♂

Black-and-white Warbler *Mniotilta varia*

DATE   LOCATION

Black-throated Blue Warbler *Dendroica caerulescens*

DATE   LOCATION

Cerulean Warbler *Dendroica cerulea*

DATE   LOCATION

Blackburnian Warbler *Dendroica fusca*

DATE   LOCATION

Black-and-white Warbler

immature ♀

breeding adult ♂

♀

♀

Black-throated Blue Warbler

♂

Appalachians ♂
cairnsi

Cerulean Warbler

immature ♀

adult ♂

♀

breeding ♀

fall adult ♂

breeding adult ♂

immature ♀

Blackburnian Warbler

Black-throated Gray Warbler *Dendroica nigrescens*

DATE   LOCATION

Townsend's Warbler *Dendroica townsendi*

DATE   LOCATION

Hermit Warbler *Dendroica occidentalis*

DATE   LOCATION

Black-throated Green Warbler *Dendroica virens*

DATE   LOCATION

Golden-cheeked Warbler *Dendroica chrysoparia*

DATE   LOCATION

Black-throated Gray Warbler

adult ♀

adult ♂

adult ♀

Townsend's Warbler

adult ♂

Townsend's x Hermit hybrid

adult ♂

adult ♀

adult ♂

Hermit Warbler

t ♀

Black-throated Green Warbler

adult ♂

Golden-cheeked Warbler

adult ♀

adult ♂

immature females

Golden-cheeked

Black-throated Green

Townsend's

Hermit

Grace's Warbler *Dendroica graciae*

DATE LOCATION

Yellow-throated Warbler *Dendroica dominica*

DATE LOCATION

Kirtland's Warbler *Dendroica kirtlandii*

DATE LOCATION

Prairie Warbler *Dendroica discolor*

DATE LOCATION

Yellow-throated Warbler

yellow-lored *dominica* ♂

white-lored *albilora* ♂

♀

Grace's Warbler

♂

immature ♀

Kirtland's Warbler

♀

♂

♀

Prairie Warbler

♂

immature ♀

Bay-breasted Warbler *Dendroica castanea*

DATE   LOCATION

Blackpoll Warbler *Dendroica striata*

DATE   LOCATION

Pine Warbler *Dendroica pinus*

DATE   LOCATION

Palm Warbler *Dendroica palmarum*

DATE   LOCATION

Bay-breasted Warbler

fall ♂

immature ♀

breeding ♀

breeding adult ♂

Blackpoll Warbler

fall

breeding ♀

breeding ♂

Pine Warbler

adult ♀

adult ♂

immature ♀

immature ♂

Palm Warbler

eastern breeding *hypochrysea*

western breeding *palmarum*

western fall *palmarum*

Yellow Warbler *Dendroica petechia*

DATE   LOCATION

Mourning Warbler *Oporornis philadelphia*

DATE   LOCATION

MacGillivray's Warbler *Oporornis tolmiei*

DATE   LOCATION

Connecticut Warbler *Oporornis agilis*

DATE   LOCATION

Yellow Warbler

♀

immature ♀

♂

immature ♀

♀

immature ♂

Mourning Warbler

♂

immature ♀

♀

MacGillivray's Warbler

♂

♀

immature

Connecticut Warbler

♂

Kentucky Warbler *Oporornis formosus*

DATE   LOCATION

Canada Warbler *Wilsonia canadensis*

DATE   LOCATION

Wilson's Warbler *Wilsonia pusilla*

DATE   LOCATION

Hooded Warbler *Wilsonia citrina*

DATE   LOCATION

Kentucky Warbler

♂

Canada Warbler

immature ♀

adult ♂

Wilson's Warbler

♀

♂

Hooded Warbler

adult ♀

adult ♂

immature ♀

Worm-eating Warbler *Helmitheros vermivorus*

DATE   LOCATION

Swainson's Warbler *Limnothlypis swainsonii*

DATE   LOCATION

Ovenbird *Seiurus aurocapillus*

DATE   LOCATION

Louisiana Waterthrush *Seiurus motacilla*

DATE   LOCATION

Northern Waterthrush *Seiurus noveboracensis*

DATE   LOCATION

Worm-eating Warbler

Swainson's Warbler

Ovenbird

Louisiana Waterthrush

Northern Waterthrush

paler

Common Yellowthroat *Geothlypis trichas*

DATE   LOCATION

Gray-crowned Yellowthroat *Geothlypis poliocephala*

DATE   LOCATION

Fan-tailed Warbler *Euthlypis lachrymosa*

DATE   LOCATION

Golden-crowned Warbler *Basileuterus culicivorus*

DATE   LOCATION

Rufous-capped Warbler *Basileuterus rufifrons*

DATE   LOCATION

Yellow-breasted Chat *Icteria virens*

DATE   LOCATION

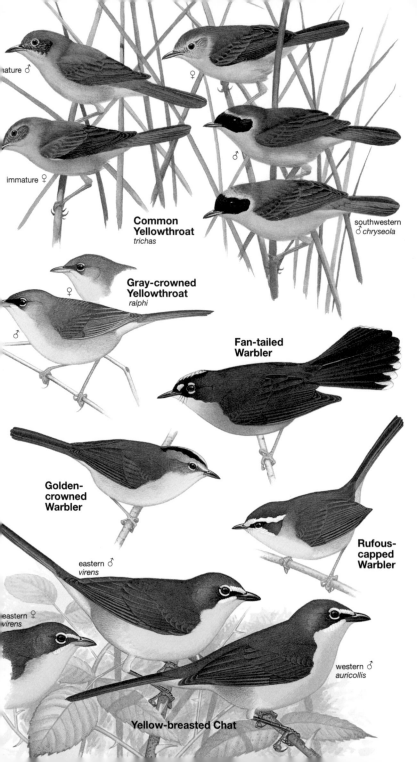

immature ♂

♀

immature ♀

Common Yellowthroat
trichas

southwestern ♂ *chryseola*

♀

♂

Gray-crowned Yellowthroat
ralphi

Fan-tailed Warbler

Golden-crowned Warbler

Rufous-capped Warbler

eastern ♂
virens

eastern ♀
virens

western ♂
auricollis

Yellow-breasted Chat

American Redstart *Setophaga ruticilla*

DATE   LOCATION

Slate-throated Redstart *Myioborus miniatus*

DATE   LOCATION

Painted Redstart *Myioborus pictus*

DATE   LOCATION

Red-faced Warbler *Cardellina rubrifrons*

DATE   LOCATION

Olive Warbler (Family Peucedramidae)

Olive Warbler *Peucedramus taeniatus*

DATE   LOCATION

American Redstart

♀

1st spring ♂

adult ♂

Slate-throated Redstart

Painted Redstart

juvenile

Red-faced Warbler

♂

adult ♂

Olive Warbler

♀

1st spring ♂

1st fall

Tanagers (Family Thraupidae)

Summer Tanager *Piranga rubra*

DATE   LOCATION

Hepatic Tanager *Piranga flava*

DATE   LOCATION

Scarlet Tanager *Piranga olivacea*

DATE   LOCATION

Western Tanager *Piranga ludoviciana*

DATE   LOCATION

Flame-colored Tanager *Piranga bidentata*

DATE   LOCATION

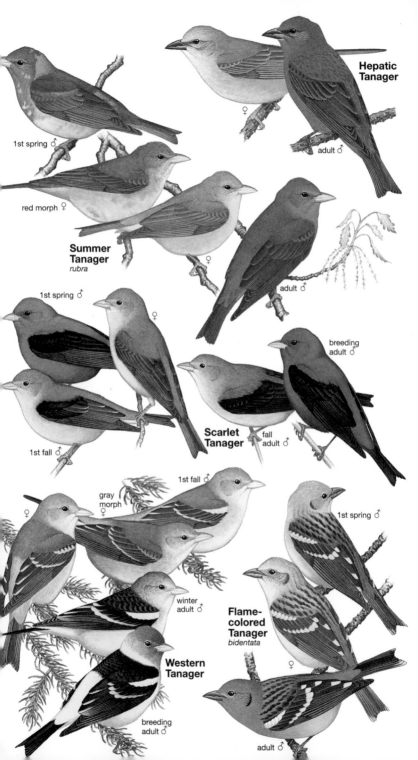

Hepatic Tanager

adult ♂

1st spring ♂

red morph ♀

Summer Tanager
rubra

♀

adult ♂

1st spring ♂

♀

breeding adult ♂

1st fall ♂

Scarlet Tanager

fall adult ♂

♀

gray morph ♀

1st fall ♂

winter adult ♂

1st spring ♂

Flame-colored Tanager
bidentata

♀

Western Tanager

breeding adult ♂

adult ♂

Stripe-headed Tanager *Spindalis zena*

DATE   LOCATION

Bananaquits (Family Coerebidae)

Bananaquit *Coereba flaveola*

DATE   LOCATION

Emberizids (Family Emberizidae)

White-collared Seedeater *Sporophila torqueola*

DATE   LOCATION

Black-faced Grassquit *Tiaris bicolor*

DATE   LOCATION

Yellow-faced Grassquit *Tiaris olivacea*

DATE   LOCATION

♂ zena

**Stripe-headed
Tanager**

♂ townsendi

♂ townsendi

♀ townsendi

♂ townsendi

**White-collared
Seedeater**
sharpei

juvenile

adult

Bananaquit
bahamensis

♀

1st
winter ♂

adult ♂

**Black-faced
Grassquit**

♀

t Indies
cea

**Yellow-faced
Grassquit**

♂

mainland
pusilla

♀

♂

adult ♂

Olive Sparrow *Arremonops rufivirgatus*

DATE   LOCATION

Green-tailed Towhee *Pipilo chlorurus*

DATE   LOCATION

California Towhee *Pipilo crissalis*

DATE   LOCATION

Canyon Towhee *Pipilo fuscus*

DATE   LOCATION

Abert's Towhee *Pipilo aberti*

DATE   LOCATION

juvenile

Olive Sparrow

spring

Green-tailed Towhee

fall

juvenile

juvenile

California Towhee

Canyon Towhee

Abert's Towhee

Eastern Towhee *Pipilo erythrophthalmus*

DATE   LOCATION

Spotted Towhee *Pipilo maculatus*

DATE   LOCATION

Eastern Towhee *erythrophthalmus*

juvenile

Florida ♂ *alleni*

♀

♂

Spotted Towhee

♀ *arcticus*

♂ *arcticus*

♂ *montanus*

♀ *montanus*

♀ *oregonus*

♂ *oregonus*

♀ *megalonyx*

juvenile *oregonus*

♂ *megalonyx*

Eastern

Spotted

erythrophthalmus *alleni* *arcticus* *montanus* *megalonyx* *oregonus*

Bachman's Sparrow *Aimophila aestivalis*

DATE   LOCATION

Botteri's Sparrow *Aimophila botterii*

DATE   LOCATION

Cassin's Sparrow *Aimophila cassinii*

DATE   LOCATION

illinoensis

Bachman's Sparrow

juvenile
illinoensis

aestivalis

Botteri's Sparrow
arizonae

juvenile

Cassin's Sparrow

juvenile

Rufous-winged Sparrow *Aimophila carpalis*

DATE   LOCATION

Rufous-crowned Sparrow *Aimophila ruficeps*

DATE   LOCATION

American Tree Sparrow *Spizella arborea*

DATE   LOCATION

Field Sparrow *Spizella pusilla*

DATE   LOCATION

Rufous-winged Sparrow

juvenile

Rufous-crowned Sparrow

coastal

interior
eremoeca

coastal
juvenile

juvenile

breeding

winter

American Tree Sparrow

Field Sparrow

western
arenacea

eastern juvenile
pusilla

eastern
pusilla

Chipping Sparrow *Spizella passerina*

DATE   LOCATION

Clay-colored Sparrow *Spizella pallida*

DATE   LOCATION

Brewer's Sparrow *Spizella breweri*

DATE   LOCATION

breeding

Chipping Sparrow

winter

juvenile

1st winter

immature

juvenile

breeding

Clay-colored Sparrow

juvenile

Brewer's Sparrow
breweri

Lark Sparrow *Chondestes grammacus*

DATE   LOCATION

Black-chinned Sparrow *Spizella atrogularis*

DATE   LOCATION

Black-throated Sparrow *Amphispiza bilineata*

DATE   LOCATION

Five-striped Sparrow *Aimophila quinquestriata*

DATE   LOCATION

Sage Sparrow *Amphispiza belli*

DATE   LOCATION

Lark Sparrow

juvenile

ck-chinned rrow

breeding ♀

breeding ♂

juvenile

Black-throated Sparrow

juvenile

-striped rrow

coastal *belli*

Sage Sparrow

interior *nevadensis*

interior juvenile *nevadensis*

Grasshopper Sparrow *Ammodramus savannarum*

DATE   LOCATION

Baird's Sparrow *Ammodramus bairdii*

DATE   LOCATION

Henslow's Sparrow *Ammodramus henslowii*

DATE   LOCATION

Grasshopper Sparrow

summer *perpallidus*

floridanus

juvenile *pratensis*

fall *pratensis*

fall *ammolegus*

Orange Bishop ♀
for comparison

Baird's Sparrow

Henslow's Sparrow

juvenile

juvenile

Saltmarsh Sharp-tailed Sparrow *Ammodramus caudacutus*

DATE   LOCATION

Le Conte's Sparrow *Ammodramus leconteii*

DATE   LOCATION

Nelson's Sharp-tailed Sparrow *Ammodramus nelsoni*

DATE   LOCATION

Seaside Sparrow *Ammodramus maritimus*

DATE   LOCATION

Saltmarsh Sharp-tailed Sparrow

Le Conte's Sparrow

juvenile

juvenile

subvirgatus

nelsoni

nelsoni

Nelson's Sharp-tailed Sparrow

juvenile *nelsoni*

maritimus

fisheri

juvenile *maritimus*

nigrescens

mirabilis

Seaside Sparrow

Fox Sparrow *Passerella iliaca*

DATE   LOCATION

Lark Bunting *Calamospiza melanocorys*

DATE   LOCATION

Savannah Sparrow *Passerculus sandwichensis*

DATE   LOCATION

Fox Sparrow

iliaca

schistacea

stephensi

unalaschcensis

fuliginosa

Lark Bunting

breeding ♂

early spring ♂

winter ♂

Savannah Sparrow

nevadensis

"Ipswich Sparrow" *princeps*

beldingi

"Large-billed Sparrow" *rostratus*

Lincoln's Sparrow *Melospiza lincolnii*

DATE   LOCATION

Song Sparrow *Melospiza melodia*

DATE   LOCATION

Vesper Sparrow *Pooecetes gramineus*

DATE   LOCATION

Swamp Sparrow *Melospiza georgiana*

DATE   LOCATION

Lincoln's Sparrow

juvenile

melodia

juvenile *melodia*

heermanni

Song Sparrow

maxima

morphna

saltonis

Vesper Sparrow

breeding

Swamp Sparrow

winter adult

juvenile

immature

Harris's Sparrow *Zonotrichia querula*

DATE··LOCATION

White-throated Sparrow *Zonotrichia albicollis*

DATE··LOCATION

White-crowned Sparrow *Zonotrichia leucophrys*

DATE··LOCATION

Golden-crowned Sparrow *Zonotrichia atricapilla*

DATE··LOCATION

Harris's Sparrow

breeding

winter adult

winter adult

immature

White-throated Sparrow

tan-striped morph

white-striped morph

juvenile

White-crowned Sparrow

adult *gambelii*

juvenile *gambelii*

adult *leucophrys*

adult *nuttalli*

immature *leucophrys*

Golden-crowned Sparrow

juvenile

immature

breeding

winter adult

Dark-eyed Junco *Junco hyemalis*

DATE   LOCATION

Yellow-eyed Junco *Junco phaeonotus*

DATE   LOCATION

"Oregon"
thurberi
♀
♂

"Slate-colored"
hyemalis
♀
♂

juvenile

"White-winged"
aikeni
♂

Dark-eyed Junco

"Slate-colored" ♂

"Pink-sided"
mearnsi
♂

"Gray-headed"
races

caniceps ♂

dorsalis ♂

Yellow-eyed Junco

juvenile

Chestnut-collared Longspur *Calcarius ornatus*

DATE   LOCATION

McCown's Longspur *Calcarius mccownii*

DATE   LOCATION

Chestnut-collared Longspur

breeding ♂

winter ♂

winter ♀

McCown's Longspur

breeding ♂

breeding ♀

winter ♀

winter ♂

juvenile

Smith's Longspur *Calcarius pictus*

DATE   LOCATION

Lapland Longspur *Calcarius lapponicus*

DATE   LOCATION

Smith's Longspur

breeding ♂

breeding ♀

winter ♂

Lapland Longspur

breeding ♂

breeding ♀

winter ♂

winter ♀

juvenile

buffy fall ♀

Snow Bunting *Plectrophenax nivalis*

DATE   LOCATION

McKay's Bunting *Plectrophenax hyperboreus*

DATE   LOCATION

Yellow-breasted Bunting *Emberiza aureola*

DATE   LOCATION

Gray Bunting *Emberiza variabilis*

DATE   LOCATION

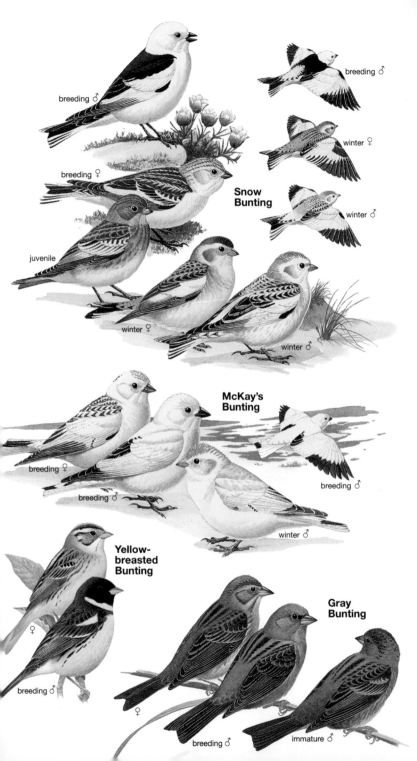

Snow Bunting

breeding ♂

breeding ♂

winter ♀

breeding ♀

winter ♂

juvenile

winter ♀

winter ♂

McKay's Bunting

breeding ♀

breeding ♂

breeding ♂

winter ♂

Yellow-breasted Bunting

♀

breeding ♂

Gray Bunting

breeding ♂

immature ♂

Reed Bunting *Emberiza schoeniclus*

DATE   LOCATION

Pallas's Bunting *Emberiza pallasi*

DATE   LOCATION

Little Bunting *Emberiza pusilla*

DATE   LOCATION

Rustic Bunting *Emberiza rustica*

DATE   LOCATION

fall adult ♂

Reed Bunting
pyrrhulina

♀

breeding ♂

♀

breeding ♂

Little Bunting

mature

breeding ♂

Pallas's Bunting

Rustic Bunting

♀

breeding ♂

Cardinals (Family Cardinalidae)

Rose-breasted Grosbeak *Pheucticus ludovicianus*

DATE   LOCATION

Black-headed Grosbeak *Pheucticus melanocephalus*

DATE   LOCATION

Crimson-collared Grosbeak *Rhodothraupis celaeno*

DATE   LOCATION

Yellow Grosbeak *Pheucticus chrysopeplus*

DATE   LOCATION

Rose-breasted Grosbeak

breeding adult ♂

breeding adult ♂

winter adult ♂

1st fall ♂

1st spring ♂

♀

Black-headed Grosbeak

♀

breeding adult ♂

1st fall ♂

Crimson-collared Grosbeak

adult ♀

adult ♂

Yellow Grosbeak

adult ♂

adult ♀

Northern Cardinal *Cardinalis cardinalis*

DATE   LOCATION

Pyrrhuloxia *Cardinalis sinuatus*

DATE   LOCATION

Dickcissel *Spiza americana*

DATE   LOCATION

Blue Grosbeak *Guiraca caerulea*

DATE   LOCATION

Northern Cardinal

♂

♀

juvenile ♂

Pyrrhuloxia

♀

♂

Dickcissel

breeding ♂

breeding ♀

winter adult ♂

immature ♂

immature ♀

Blue Grosbeak

breeding adult ♂

♀

immature

1st spring ♂

Indigo Bunting *Passerina cyanea*

DATE   LOCATION

Lazuli Bunting *Passerina amoena*

DATE   LOCATION

Painted Bunting *Passerina ciris*

DATE   LOCATION

Varied Bunting *Passerina versicolor*

DATE   LOCATION

Blue Bunting *Cyanocompsa parellina*

DATE   LOCATION

Indigo Bunting

winter adult ♂

fall

♀

1st spring ♂

breeding adult ♂

Lazuli Bunting

...ling ♂

1st spring ♂

♀

juvenile

adult ♂

Painted Bunting

♀

Varied Bunting

breeding adult ♂

winter adult ♂

♀

Blue Bunting

♀

adult ♂

Blackbirds (Familiy Icteridae)

Bobolink *Dolichonyx oryzivorus*

DATE   LOCATION

Eastern Meadowlark *Sturnella magna*

DATE   LOCATION

Western Meadowlark *Sturnella neglecta*

DATE   LOCATION

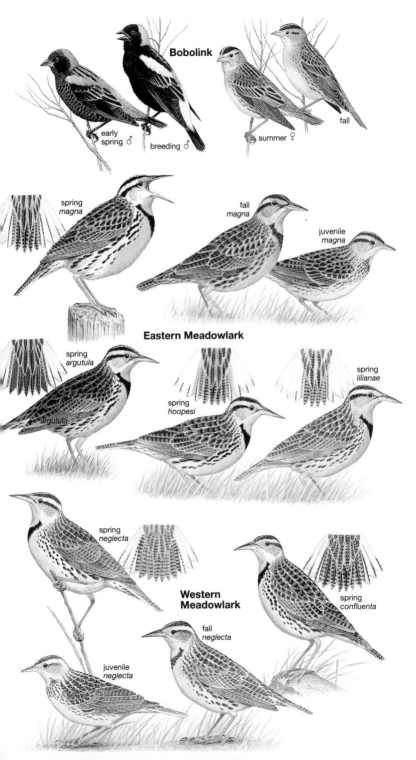

Bobolink

early spring ♂

breeding ♂

summer ♀

fall

spring
magna

fall
magna

juvenile
magna

Eastern Meadowlark

spring
argutula

argutula

spring
hoopesi

spring
lilianae

spring *neglecta*

Western Meadowlark

spring
confluenta

fall
neglecta

juvenile
neglecta

Yellow-headed Blackbird *Xanthocephalus xanthocephalus*

DATE   LOCATION

Red-winged Blackbird *Agelaius phoeniceus*

DATE   LOCATION

Tricolored Blackbird *Agelaius tricolor*

DATE   LOCATION

spring adult ♂

1st winter ♂

juvenile

Yellow-headed Blackbird

spring adult ♂

1st year ♂

♀

immature ♀

Red-winged Blackbird

"Bicolored Blackbird"

adult ♂

adult ♂

Tricolored Blackbird

breeding ♂

♀

Common Grackle *Quiscalus quiscula*

DATE   LOCATION

Boat-tailed Grackle *Quiscalus major*

DATE   LOCATION

Great-tailed Grackle *Quiscalus mexicanus*

DATE   LOCATION

Common Grackle

purple ♂
quiscula

bronze ♂
versicolor

juvenile

juvenile ♀

juvenile ♂

♀

Boat-tailed Grackle
major

western
Gulf
coast

♂

juvenile ♀

Great-tailed Grackle

♀

♂

western ♀
nelsoni

Rusty Blackbird *Euphagus carolinus*

DATE · · · · · · · · · · · LOCATION

Brewer's Blackbird *Euphagus cyanocephalus*

DATE · · · · · · · · · · · LOCATION

Shiny Cowbird *Molothrus bonariensis*

DATE · · · · · · · · · · · LOCATION

Brown-headed Cowbird *Molothrus ater*

DATE · · · · · · · · · · · LOCATION

Bronzed Cowbird *Molothrus aeneus*

DATE · · · · · · · · · · · LOCATION

Rusty Blackbird

fall ♀

fall ♂

breeding ♀

breeding ♂

Brewer's Blackbird

fall variant ♂

♂

♀

Shiny Cowbird

♀

♂

Brown-headed Cowbird

juvenile

♀

♂

southwestern ♀ *loyei*

Bronzed Cowbird *aeneus*

juvenile

♂

♀

Orchard Oriole *Icterus spurius*

DATE   LOCATION

Hooded Oriole *Icterus cucullatus*

DATE   LOCATION

Baltimore Oriole *Icterus galbula*

DATE   LOCATION

Bullock's Oriole *Icterus bullockii*

DATE   LOCATION

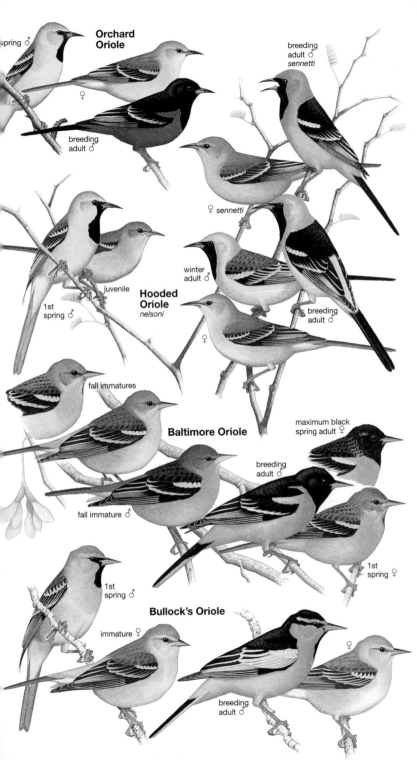

spring ♂

Orchard Oriole

♀

breeding adult ♂

breeding adult ♂ *sennetti*

♀ *sennetti*

1st spring ♂

juvenile

Hooded Oriole
nelsoni

winter adult ♂

breeding adult ♂

♀

fall immatures

Baltimore Oriole

maximum black spring adult ♀

breeding adult ♂

fall immature ♂

1st spring ♀

1st spring ♂

immature ♀

Bullock's Oriole

♀

breeding adult ♂

Black-vented Oriole *Icterus wagleri*

DATE................................LOCATION...

....

....

Streak-backed Oriole *Icterus pustulatus*

DATE................................LOCATION...

....

....

Altamira Oriole *Icterus gularis*

DATE................................LOCATION...

....

....

Audubon's Oriole *Icterus graduacauda*

DATE................................LOCATION...

....

....

Spot-breasted Oriole *Icterus pectoralis*

DATE................................LOCATION...

....

....

Scott's Oriole *Icterus parisorum*

DATE................................LOCATION...

....

....

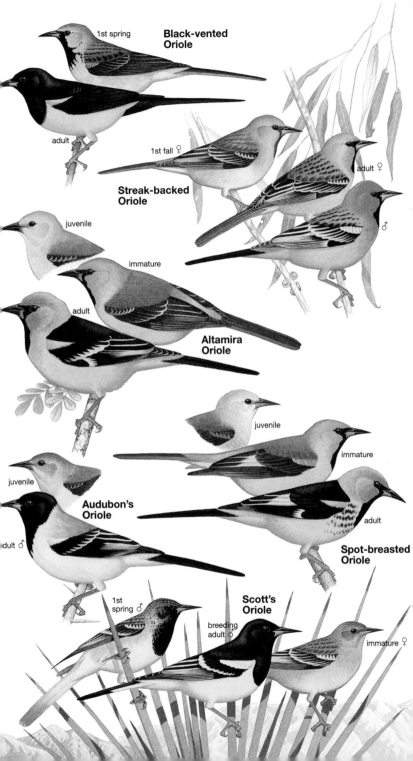

Black-vented Oriole

1st spring

adult

Streak-backed Oriole

1st fall ♀

adult ♀

♂

juvenile

immature

adult

Altamira Oriole

juvenile

immature

adult

Audubon's Oriole

juvenile

adult ♂

Spot-breasted Oriole

1st spring ♂

Scott's Oriole

breeding adult ♂

immature ♀

Finches (Family Fringillidae)

Oriental Greenfinch *Carduelis sinica*

DATE··LOCATION···

Brambling *Fringilla montifringilla*

DATE··LOCATION···

Common Chaffinch *Fringilla coelebs*

DATE··LOCATION···

Gray-crowned Rosy-Finch *Leucosticte tephrocotis*

DATE··LOCATION···

Brown-capped Rosy-Finch *Leucosticte australis*

DATE··LOCATION···

Black Rosy-Finch *Leucosticte atrata*

DATE··LOCATION···

Oriental Greenfinch

adult ♂

adult ♀

juvenile

Brambling

breeding ♂

fall ♂

♀

Common Chaffinch

♀

♂

Gray-crowned Rosy-Finch

juvenile

interior

breeding ♂

Pribilofs winter ♂ *umbrina*

"Hepburn's" winter ♂ *littoralis*

Brown-capped Rosy-Finch

breeding ♀

breeding ♂

Black Rosy-Finch

breeding ♀

breeding ♂

Purple Finch *Carpodacus purpureus*

DATE   LOCATION

Cassin's Finch *Carpodacus cassinii*

DATE   LOCATION

House Finch *Carpodacus mexicanus*

DATE   LOCATION

Common Rosefinch *Carpodacus erythrinus*

DATE   LOCATION

♀ *californicus*

Purple Finch

♀ *purpureus*

Pacific coast
adult ♂
californicus

eastern adult ♂
purpureus

Cassin's Finch

adult ♀

adult ♂

typical ♂

House Finch

variant ♂

♀

Common Rosefinch

♀

adult ♂

Red Crossbill *Loxia curvirostra*

DATE   LOCATION

White-winged Crossbill *Loxia leucoptera*

DATE   LOCATION

Pine Grosbeak *Pinicola enucleator*

DATE   LOCATION

variant ♂

juvenile

Red Crossbill

northern *minor* ♀

typical ♀

typical ♂

southwestern *stricklandi* ♂

immature ♂

juvenile

White-winged Crossbill

♀

winter adult ♂

♀

adult ♂

russet variant

Pine Grosbeak

Pine Siskin *Carduelis pinus*

DATE   LOCATION

American Goldfinch *Carduelis tristis*

DATE   LOCATION

Lesser Goldfinch *Carduelis psaltria*

DATE   LOCATION

Lawrence's Goldfinch *Carduelis lawrencei*

DATE   LOCATION

Pine Siskin

juvenile

American Goldfinch

breeding ♀

breeding ♂

winter adult ♂

winter ♀

juvenile

♀

Lesser Goldfinch

ack-backed ♂

pale ♀

en-backed ♂

immature ♂

Lawrence's Goldfinch

winter ♀

winter ♂

breeding ♂

juvenile

Common Redpoll *Carduelis flammea*

DATE   LOCATION

Hoary Redpoll *Carduelis hornemanni*

DATE   LOCATION

Evening Grosbeak *Coccothraustes vespertinus*

DATE   LOCATION

Hawfinch *Coccothraustes coccothraustes*

DATE   LOCATION

Eurasian Bullfinch *Pyrrhula pyrrhula*

DATE   LOCATION

Common Redpoll *flammea*
- juvenile
- breeding ♀
- breeding ♂
- winter ♀
- winter ♂

Hoary Redpoll
- winter ♀ *exilipes*
- winter ♂ *hornemanni*
- winter ♂ *exilipes*

Evening Grosbeak
- ♂
- ♀
- breeding ♂
- juvenile
- breeding ♀

Hawfinch
- breeding ♂

Eurasian Bullfinch *cassinii*
- ♀
- ♂

Old World Sparrows (Family Passeridae)

House Sparrow *Passer domesticus*

DATE   LOCATION

Eurasian Tree Sparrow *Passer montanus*

DATE   LOCATION

Estrildid Finches (Family Estrildidae)

Nutmeg Mannikin *Lonchura punctulata*

DATE   LOCATION

Weavers (Family Ploceidae)

Orange Bishop *Euplectes franciscanus*

DATE   LOCATION

fall ♂

breeding ♂

♀

House Sparrow

Eurasian Tree Sparrow

juvenile

displaying

breeding ♂

Orange Bishop

Nutmeg Mannikin

nile

♀

Index

The main entry for each species is listed in **boldface** type and refers to the text page opposite the illustration.

Artists' Credits

Jonathan K. Alderfer
pages 27-heads, 29, 31-except Northern Fulmar, 35-Dark-rumped and Murphy's petrels, 37-molting Pink-footed Shearwater, 39-Wedge-tailed Shearwater, Bulwer's Petrel, left Short-tailed Shearwater, and heads, 41-top right comparison figures, 49, 153, 171-flying Black Turnstone, 181, 183, 225-flying winter Dovekie, 227-Long-billed Murrelet, 233-flying Rhinoceros Auklet, 237 (with Schmitt), 339-female Blue-gray Gnatcatcher tail, 359-Common Myna.

David Beadle
pages 289-293, 311-Philadelphia and Warbling vireos, 335-western Winter Wren, 371-Crescent-chested Warbler, 381-fall male Bay-breasted Warbler, 391-Red-faced Warbler.

Peter Burke
pages 65-Glossy (except flying) and White-faced ibises, 287-Cuban Pewee and smaller Olive-sided Flycatcher, 297, 303-Piratic and Variegated flycatchers, 307-Thick-billed Vireo, 309-Gray Vireo, 353-White-throated Robin, 389-except Common Yellowthroat, 393, 395-adult male White-collared Seedeater and Yellow-faced Grassquit, 397, 399, 429-Crimson-collared Grosbeak, 441-Shiny Cowbird, 443, 445.

Marc R. Hanson
pages 31-Northern Fulmar, 35-Mottled, Stejneger's, and Cook's petrels, 37-except molting Pink-footed Shearwater, 39-Flesh-footed, Sooty, and right Short-tailed shearwaters, 41-except top right comparison figures, 43, 45, 145-149.

Cynthia J. House
pages 67-except immature Whooper Swan, 69-73, 75-except flying Muscovy Duck, 77-except female American Black Duck, 79-95, 97-except Egyptian Goose, 98-101.

H. Jon Janosik
pages 25, 27-except heads, 47, 51-55, 159, 169.

Donald L. Malick
pages 103-105, 109-except Steller's Sea-Eagle and third year Bald Eagle, 111-except three flying juveniles, 113-perched figures, except adult Common Black-Hawk, 117, 119-except dark morph Ferruginous and adult and dark juvenile White-tailed hawks, 121-Crested Caracara and perched Aplomado Falcon, 123-all perched figures and upper flying American Kestrel, 125, 239, 249-257, 273-285.

Killian Mullarney
pages 157, 179, 185, 188-Little Ringed Plover.

John P. O'Neill
pages 271-trogons, 303-Rose-throated Becard, 321, 327-331.

Michael O'Brien
page 33.

Kent Pendleton
pages 107, 126-except Hook-billed Kite, 127-129, 131-except Chachalaca and flying Chukar, 133-143.

Diane Pierce
pages 57, 59, 61-except Little Egret, 63, 65-White, Scarlet, and flying Glossy ibises and Roseate Spoonbill, 151, 401-407, 409-except Orange Bishop, 411-Seaside Sparrow, 413, 415-except Vesper Sparrow, 417, 419-except flying Dark-eyed Junco, 421, 423, 425-except Yellow-breasted Bunting, 427, 429-except Crimson-collared Grosbeak, 431, 433, 447-except Common Chaffinch, 449-455.

John C. Pitcher
pages 155, 161-except Common Redshank, 163, 165, 171-except flying Black Turnstone, 175, 177.

H. Douglas Pratt
cover, pages 235, 245, 247, 265-except immature Green Violet-ear, Lucifer Hummingbird, and Green-breasted Mango, 267-except Xantus's Hummingbird, 269-except wing figures, 271-hummingbirds, 287-except small Olive-sided Flycatcher and Cuban Pewee, 295, 299, 301, 303-except Piratic and Variegated

fly-catchers and Rose-throated Becard, 305-except Brown Shrike, 307-except Thick-billed Vireo, 309-except Gray Vireo, 311-except Philadelphia and Warbling vireos, 313, 315-except Island Scrub-Jay and adult Mexican Jays, 317, 319, 323-except Common House-Martin, 325, 333, 335-except western Winter Wren, 337, 339-except female Blue-gray Gnatcatcher tail, 341-except Lanceolated Warbler, 347, 351-except Fieldfare and Redwing, 353-except White-throated Robin, 355, 359-except Common Myna, 361-except Siberian Accentor, 363-American, tail of Sprague's, and Red-throated pipits, 365-369, 371-except Crescent-chested Warbler, 373-379, 381-except fall male Bay-breasted Warbler, 383-387, 389-Common Yellowthroat, 391-except Red-faced Warbler, 395-Bananaquit, Black-faced Grassquit, and female and first winter male White-collared Seedeater, 437, 439, 441-except Shiny Cowbird.

David Quinn
pages 21, 23, 61-Little Egret, 161-Common Redshank, 187-Common Redshank, 305-Brown Shrike, 323-Common House-Martin, 341-Lance-olated Warbler, 343, 345, 351- Field-fare and Redwing, 361-Siberian Accentor, 363-Sprague's (except tail), Olive-backed, and Pechora pipits, 425-Yellow-breasted Bunting, 447-Common Chaffinch.

Chuck Ripper
pages 225-except flying winter Dovekie, 227-except Long-billed Murrelet, 229, 231, 233-except flying Rhinoceros Auklet, 259, 261-except *arizonae* Whip-poor-will tail.

N. John Schmitt
pages 67-immature Whooper Swan, 75-flying Muscovy Ducks, 77-female American Black Duck, 97-Egyptian Goose, 109-Steller's Sea-Eagle and third year Bald Eagle, 111- three flying juveniles, 113-adult Common Black-Hawk and all flight figures, 115, 119-dark morph Ferruginous and adult and dark juvenile White-tailed hawks, 121-Hobby and flying Aplomado Falcons, 123-all flight figures except upper American Kestrel, 126-Hook-billed Kite, 131-Chacha-laca and flying Chukar, 167- Little, Bristle-thighed, and Eurasian curlews, 186- Little Curlew, 237 (with Alderfer), 241, 243, 263, 315-Island Scrub-Jay and adult Mexican Jays, 357, 409-Orange Bishop, 411-except Seaside Sparrow, 415-Vesper Sparrow, 419-flying Dark-eyed Junco, 457.

Thomas R. Schultz
pages 173, 191-223, 349, 395-Stripe-headed Tanager, 435.

Daniel S. Smith
pages 167-Eskimo, Long-billed, and Far Eastern curlews and Whimbrel, 186-except Little Curlew, 187-except Common Redshank, 188-except Little Ringed Plover, 189.

Sophie Webb
pages 261-*arizonae* Whip-poor-will tail, 265- immature Green Violet-ear, Green-breasted Mango and Lucifer Hummingbird, 267-Xantus's Hummingbird, 269-wing figures.

Acknowledgments

We wish to thank Mel M. Baughman for assisting in the development of this book. The Book Division also wishes to express its gratitude to the following individuals and organizations for their contributions: David Agro; Jon Barlow; Louis Bevier; the Department of Ornithology at the British Museum; Dawn Burke; Steven W. Cardiff; Carla Cicero; Rene Corado; Donna L. Dittmann; Peter J. Dunn; Field Museum of Natural History, Chicago; Dr. Clemency Fisher; John W. Fitzpatrick; Kimball L. Garrett; Daniel D. Gibson; Jon S. Greenlaw; Mary Gustafson; J.B. Hallett; Jr.; Paul M. Hill; Phill Holder; Steve N.G. Howell; Frank Iwen; Alvaro Jaramillo; Joseph R. Jehl; Jr.; Ned K. Johnson; Colin Jones; Marianne G. Koszorus; Los Angeles County Museum of Natural History; Dr. Malcolm Largen; Greg Lasley; Nick Lethaby; Liverpool Museum, England; Tim Loseby; Laura Martin; Doug McRae; Dominic Mitchell; Glen Murphy; Museum of Vertebrate Zoology, University of California, Berkeley; Tony Parker; Brian Patteson; Mark Peck; Paul Prior; Peter Pyle; Mark Robbins; Royal Ontario Museum; San Diego Natural History Museum; Larry Sansone; Thomas Schulenberg; David Sibley; Doug Stotz; Sherman Suter; Philip Unitt; George Wallace; Western Foundation of Vertebrate Zoology; David W. Willard; Louise Zemaitis; and Kevin Zimmer.

Published by the National Geographic Society

John M. Fahey, Jr.	*President and Chief Executive Officer*
Gilbert M. Grosvenor	*Chairman of the Board*
Nina D. Hoffman	*Senior Vice President*

Prepared by the Book Division

William R. Gray	*Vice President and Director*
Charles Kogod	*Assistant Director*
Barbara A. Payne	*Editorial Director and Managing Editor*
David Griffin	*Design Director*

Consultants for this book

Jon L. Dunn, *Chief Consultant*

Jonathan K. Alderfer, *Art Consultant and General Consultant*

Staff for this book

Dale-Marie Herring, *Editor*

Lyle Rosbotham, *Art Director*

Gillian Carol Dean, *Designer*

R. Gary Colbert, *Production Director*

Richard S. Wain, *Production Project Manager*

Peggy Candore, *Assistant to the Director*

Alexander L. Cohn, Johnna M. Rizzo, Sandy Leonard, *Staff Assistants*

Mark A. Wentling, *Indexer*

Manufacturing and Quality Control

George V. White, *Director*

John T. Dunn, *Associate Director*

Vincent P. Ryan, *Manager*

James J. Sorensen, *Budget Analyst*

The world's largest nonprofit scientific and educational organization, the National Geographic Society was founded in 1888 "for the increase and diffusion of geographic knowledge." Since then it has supported scientific exploration and spread information to its more than nine million members worldwide.

The National Geographic Society educates and inspires millions every day through magazines, books, television programs, videos, maps and atlases, research grants, the National Geography Bee, teacher workshops, and innovative classroom materials.

The Society is supported through membership dues and income from the sale of its educational products. Members receive NATIONAL GEOGRAPHIC magazine—the Society's official journal—discounts on Society products, and other benefits.

For more information about the National Geographic Society and its educational programs and publications, please call 1-800-NGS-LINE (647-5463), or write to the following address:

National Geographic Society
1145 17th Street N.W.
Washington, D.C. 20036-4688 U.S.A.

Visit the Society's Web site at www.nationalgeographic.com.